The *Art* AND SCIENCE OF *Success*

The Art AND SCIENCE OF Success

PROVEN STRATEGIES FROM Today's LEADING EXPERTS

SUCCESS YOU PUBLISHING
CARROLLTON, TX

© 2011 Matt Morris

Success You Publishing, Inc.
2810 Trinity Mills Road #209-142
Carrollton, TX 75006
questions@mattmorris.com

ISBN: 978-0-9830770-0-8

Printed in United States of America

Cover Design: Chris Collins
Interior Design & Layout: Ghislain Viau

Contents

Chapter 1

The Power of Manifestation

by Matt Morris

I t had been about three days since my last bath. Not that you could really even call it a bath. . . . Every two or three days I would find a gas station bathroom that would lock from the inside. I'd take off all my clothes, splash water up from the sink, soap up, and then splash water to rinse off. I remember always praying that no one would be waiting outside because the floor would be soaking wet.

I had completely run out of money. I had also run out of credit— I was approximately $30,000 in debt and couldn't even make the minimum payments on my credit cards. I had been forced to live out of my car because I couldn't afford rent and couldn't afford even $20 a night to stay in a sleazy motel. I was selling above-ground swimming pools in southern Louisiana during the two hottest months of the year and didn't get paid commissions until the pool got installed six to eight weeks later. So for two months, my Honda Civic was my home sweet home.

Sitting all alone in my car about 2:00 a.m., I was overly aware that my life had hit rock bottom. Not only because I was lonely, broke, and living out of my car, but because I had just showered naked in the rain in the church lot I was parked in. To be more accurate, I had showered under the gutter runoff from the roof of the church.

The burning question in my mind that night was, "How?" How in the world had I gotten myself into this situation? I knew I wasn't there because of a lack of effort or even a lack of intelligence. (I wasn't lazy, and I actually considered myself to be a pretty smart guy.)

After experiencing both utter failure and extreme success in my life, I have become acutely aware of what exactly manifested that situation. I'm also aware of what has now allowed me to become a self-made millionaire, travel around the world to over 50 countries, and become a best-selling author and a speaker addressing audiences of thousands every year.

What you might think caused those results were the *actions* leading up to them because, as we know, every action does produce a result. Most people focus only on the "how to's" but never seem to achieve their full potential because the decision to take proper or improper actions are a byproduct of their original intention. If the intention is not set properly, one will almost always make the wrong decisions on what actions to take, which, in turn, will lead to an undesired result.

What lies at the heart of manifesting your full potential is your intention.

What is intention? The dictionary defines it as the end or object intended; purpose. While that sounds incredibly simple, utilizing the power of intention requires truly manifesting that purpose for yourself.

An intention is your inner belief in what is already present but has simply not manifested in physical form yet. A true intention comes with the commitment and honest belief that anything else is an absolute impossibility. You see, when you're committed to a result, it's already done. Without it already being done in your mind, it cannot be considered a true intention but is simply a fleeting wish.

When it comes to achieving your result, the most simple and widely accepted model for you to follow is what we call *cause and effect*. Think of your result as your effect. Your job is to identify and create the cause that will produce your effect.

Most people naturally assume that the cause is the physical actions or the steps you need to take to get your desired effect. What I'm proposing to you here, however, is that the series of action steps is not the real cause. The actions are really part of the effect.

So the question is, then, what's the cause?

The real cause is the intention you make to create that effect in the first place. The moment you say to yourself, "let it be so," is the real cause. Without the decision, or your intention, the effect will never manifest. Your intention is ultimately what causes everything in your life to manifest.

If you want to achieve a goal, the most crucial part is to *decide* to manifest it. It doesn't matter if you feel it's out of your capabilities to achieve it. It doesn't matter if you can't see *how* you're going to achieve it. The *how* is insignificant because the universe will usually never manifest the *how* until *after* you've made the decision.

The origin of the word *decide* is actually "to cut off." Your "decision," then, should be framed in your mind as cutting off any other option other than your desired result. If failure is an option in your mind, your true intention is actually failure.

So step 1 is to *decide* . . . not to wonder if you can do it and not to think of all the reasons that are holding you back. If you want to start your own business, then decide to make it so first. If you want to get married, decide to attract a mate. Whatever it is you want out of life, make a decision and a commitment *first* and *then* work out the *how*.

If you think doubt in your head, you find doubt in the world. You see, my belief is that the universe can sense a lack of commitment to a goal. It's like those people who say they are going to *try* to do something and *see how it goes*. When you come from a place of uncertainty, or if you're wishy-washy about your goal, then the universe is not going to help you achieve it.

When you have total certainty from declaring your intention, you attract people like a magnet. When you are energized and motivated and have declared your goal to be so, that resonates in your being and the universe aligns itself to work with you to manifest your intention.

You must also realize that your subconscious mind is infinitely more powerful than your conscious mind, and that your subconscious mind controls your outcome 100%. When you are uncertain consciously about your goal, your subconscious does everything in its power to hold you back. Your subconscious acts like a computer. It accepts 100% of the data your conscious mind gives it. When your conscious mind feeds it negativity, it produces negative results for you. When your conscious mind feeds it excitement, positivity, and certainty, it produces all the energy and all the creativity it possibly can to ensure that you accomplish your intended result.

If you put out negative thoughts toward your desired outcome, you will be incongruent, and your subconscious mind will do everything in its power to sabotage your success.

If you want to achieve any goal, your first step is to declare it and then to clear out all words like "hopefully" "can't" "maybe" and the killer—"try". When someone tells me they're going to "try" to do something, I always know that they're *not* going to do it.

Such words are all signs that you lack commitment, that you don't believe in yourself, and that you're using your own power against yourself. You see, we all have the same amount of power—you just have to decide if you want to use your power negatively or positively. When you use your power negatively, you're saying, "let me be powerless." If you think weakness, you manifest weakness. If you project certainty, you manifest certainty.

"Energy flows where attention goes."

You get whatever you think about most often. Whatever you think about expands. Therefore we must constantly focus on what we want! We create our destiny by the committed focus of our intention.

Biography

Matt Morris

MATT MORRIS is the international best-selling author of *The Unemployed Millionaire.* A serial entrepreneur since the age of 18, Matt has generated tens of millions of dollars through his companies while generating over 100,000 customers in 180 countries around the world. As a dynamic speaker, best-selling author, and young success story, Matt has been featured on international radio and television and has addressed audiences in over 20 countries worldwide. Matt is widely known as one of the top Internet marketing experts and is the founder of Success You Publishing, Inc.

Contact Information

www.MattMorris.com

Chapter 2

Essential Success
A LIVING TRANSFORMATION

by Ray Blanchard, Ph.D.

*If you knew you had only a short time to live, and then it would be over,
what would you do with the rest of your life?*

This message is for individuals who desire to succeed beyond measure, and who feel an urgent need to live their true potential. That means living with purpose and passion, having the courage to dream big and go after what you really want, as if the present is all you have. This crash course on self-transformation explains several basic understandings and distinctions so you can flip the switch to your success. It is your challenge to live such wisdoms and to keep those distinctions alive.

My story may be like yours, a typical "zero to hero" scenario. It reveals lessons for a clear path to change lives for the better. It is amazing how these humble beginnings built such a solid foundation for the achievements that followed.

I am one of 12 children, the youngest of 6 sons, born to a strong-willed Mississippi farmer. My mother always stressed learning from your hardships and moving on without complaining, while giving something to your neighbors along the way. Life was a struggle for my parents, always barely making ends meet. The ultimate struggle came when I was about 12 years old, and the ravages of a tornado tearing through our little shotgun house forced us to pick up and leave the farm my father had worked since he was born some 66 years earlier.

I had been a "smart" little kid in the country school where my aunt was principal and most of the grades were in the same room. But moving to the big city, St. Louis, I was quite unprepared to compete with my classmates. Not liking that, I worked hard to prove myself, to help the family out, and to make my parents proud. I got a job in a grocery store and ran a newspaper route. I paid for my clothes and school supplies. By my second year in high school, I was able to start sports, where I learned to strive even harder and always aim to win. Taking a new job at the local hospital in the morning before school, and running two miles through the park to make it to morning classes, I became a good athlete and student. My counselors took notice of my efforts and decided to help me get into college, since my parents would not have been able to help me at all. Forging ahead with encouragement from my adviser, I finally got a break. I went to night school at Washington University in St. Louis until I earned the opportunity to go full time. One professor took special interest in me, after noticing my love for classical philosophy, and helped me get through two degrees and a fellowship to a doctoral program, where I excelled.

Two key mentors pushed and goaded me to keep moving until I graduated a doctor of philosophy in psychology after a little more than three years. My proudest moment was when my mom was able to come 2,000 miles on her first airplane flight to see the first of her brood get an advanced college degree. Since then, other mentors at significant stages of my life helped me go to the next level of success, through the wisdoms they had gained and imparted to me. The unbelievable support from these life coaches has taken me around the world in more ways than one and has stewarded me to extraordinary accomplishments and joy. I feel blessed, grateful, and passionate about giving back.

The greatest success lesson in all my experiences is to *always believe,* especially when the light is dim and there doesn't seem to be a way out. Keep your belief strong and determined to outlast the challenges. Don't ever give up on what matters. You often gain victory in the darkest hour, by that one extra burst of effort as though your life depended on it. In the race for life, it's that last stretch that gives you victory, marking the final arrival after a long journey.

The completion of a heartfelt commitment is the ultimate arrival. But the process of getting there with joy and passion is the most meaningful. If you can live your life with joy and ease while attaining satisfaction in personal, professional, and spiritual affairs, you are a success.

On your way to the top, it is important to give back and help someone else. *"Reach back and pull someone else up."* Pay it forward. This provides satisfaction for you and makes a difference in the social consciousness of the world. The yin and yang of a principled life, and the most important character traits in achieving complete success, are getting results *and* being a giver.

Four key factors are always present in my successes and usually in those of the giants we revere as well: (1) hard work, (2) knowledge, (3) attitude, and (4) love of God or the Almighty.

Hard Work

Let's face it—life can be tough. Not many successes have been authentically achieved without hard work. That does not mean that life has to be hard. It just means be prepared. Make going the extra mile a practice.

For instance, if you are exercising, do a few more minutes or add a few extra repetitions. It is well established that the greatest consistent results come from our extra efforts rather than the easy actions we start out with.

In relationships, stretch yourself and have a few more authentic conversations with loved ones and colleagues each week. You will quickly realize that you have super-powered your network of support. Support is vital to being the best you can be and to giving peak performances. Plus you tend to open up a lot more opportunities and possibilities, personally and professionally, when you reach out.

Refrain from having to be "right" in every conversation. "Being right" is a social disease, an addiction that destroys relationships on all levels. At least two or three times a week, be conscious of your impulse to dig in your heels to argue your point. Then let it go. Create win-win interactions and experiences that will uplift your friendships and open more space for everyone to grow. All will be happier and healthier for it, and it is widely believed to add a few more years to your life as well.

These acts may take more focused awareness in your relationships, but the rewards are worth it in your experience of success. You shape the consciousness landscape that surrounds you and enhance your social capital among your peers.

In addition, invest a few hours a week in personal growth and inner development activities. The value you gain accumulates and even compounds. By the end of a month, you will notice a big difference. By the end of a year, you will have invested almost a week in yourself. Remember that, after your maker, *you* are the *answer* and the key to your own success.

I strongly suggest pursuing effective empowerment seminars as well. You can learn more about yourself from such outside sources than you can ever learn from your already existing views of life. I had a true enlightenment experience in a seminar in the early years of my professional life. It was life altering, and I treasure it to this day. It could be like that for you too.

Knowledge

Knowledge is the key to power. And power is the ability to turn possibility into reality. The first principle of knowledge is to *"know thyself."* To accomplish this, you need to thoroughly examine your life and see what makes you tick. Sorting through your experiences and beliefs can tell you why you feel, think, and do what you do and why you get the results you get. Realizing this gives you access to your life script and behavior patterns at the root level, thereby allowing you to create a new blueprint for success.

Make a practice to go into deep thought a few minutes a day to specifically examine the genesis of your beliefs and make corrections that will lead to more expertise, free choice, and precise actions that create the results you want. Learn to use the "stop-look-listen" process for self-reflection and life improvement. Stop being on autopilot, just reacting. Look at life from a new angle or perspective. Listen to your heartfelt commitment rather than negative self-talk. This will help you steadily make strides toward your higher goals.

Also take time to reflect on material you read each day, examining it from different angles and understandings. Don't be a "yes" machine. Challenge ideas. This practice in discipline and critical analysis enriches your creativity and ability to invent new possibilities.

Dedicate an extra two hours a week to a hobby. It will keep you fresh and will likely play a part in the rest of your career, by adding richness and a new dimension to whatever you do. The added time per year that you put into your deeper interests and your career will give you the competitive edge to increase your chances for greatness.

Attitude

All reality is dictated by the context that supports it. Positive thoughts lead to positive attitudes and actions; negative ones lead to negative outcomes. In effect, thoughts are things. Deliberately train your attitude and thought processes to generate your desire. This is the key to flipping the switch to success.

Several years ago, one of my good friends who had a less-than-pleasant attitude came to this realization and did something about it, and it significantly shifted his business. He made a paradigm shift to accentuate the positive and eliminate the negative. He started a slogan for his company and followed it: *"I shall not complain."*

He made a point of eliminating at least a few complaints a day, noting each time he interrupted his negative thoughts. The impact of eliminating several hundred negative imprints a year altered his outlook and ultimately attracted more customers. Consider doing the same exercise for a year. Include thoughts about your job, family, neighbor, the weather, your love life, your bank account, the economy, your friends, and so forth. *"You reap what you sow."* Change your mind, and change your life.

Love of God or the Almighty

The human condition is the continuous search for meaning and fulfillment. Our spiritual reality sustains us and supports our reason for being.

To say the least, truth and meaning are a matter of interpretation. We are continuously interpreting and assessing our spiritual reality, making meaning out of it, and using our interpretations and meanings to act in ways we think will fulfill our lives.

Regardless of how we arrive at our conclusions, most great achievers agree that material success alone is meaningless, and success without fulfilling a higher purpose is emptiness.

Some of us believe there is a greater Source of life and meaning outside our own interpretation, and it is our pleasure to serve It. Some do not. We get to choose for ourselves what is true for us. Our happiness and motivation often depend on it. For me, the Almighty source of life and meaning is God.

The pursuit of meaning or truth is a personal and private matter. The sooner you begin the quest, the greater your advantage. Regardless of what you discover, the act of giving and making a difference through service seems to be the right path to finding out. It provides an empowering sense of purpose and deep satisfaction that propels us to achieve.

Contributing to world transformation and peace are popular undertakings. Healing the environment, ending hunger on the planet, or providing health needs to the sick are also possibilities. Serving your community, church, or charity are other ways to quell the thirst. Contributing a few hours of service a week will culminate in a several weeks a year giving to others and making a difference. It makes you feel good about yourself. It is life redeeming, and it powerfully affects your sense of value.

Success is determined by how well you live your life. Wealth, character, or a combination thereof are generally the measures. The risks you take, the courage you demonstrate, your ease in letting go of disappointment and pain, your ability to shift point of view and come off autopilot, your ability to think and create possibility in the face of the impossible, how you include people and bring them forward, the patience and love you express and receive, and the difference you make in others' lives are the defining factors.

Leaders possess these qualities in abundance, and in sharing them they make the difference between potential and reality. *"Having what it takes and not using it is a waste; but living such qualities can transform the world."*

After all is said and done, success is self-realization. Being real and being oneself is the most one can be. Our challenge is to strive for such completeness, so that we reach the pinnacle of human achievement and excellence. My favorite quote, *"To thine own self, be true,"* captures it succinctly.

The way of the Buddha is an exquisite example. It is the way of ease, a balance of effort and effortlessness in perfect harmony. It demonstrates integrity, which is *essential success*. The life of Jesus is a perfect model of success in action, in terms of handling challenges and relating to others. He is an example of acceptance and inclusion, never giving up, having purpose and passion, and overcoming while still loving—*a living transformation*. Together they represent our ultimate goal, which is to be whole, perfect, and complete. And that is *essential success—a living transformation*.

Biography

Dr. Ray Blanchard

DR. RAY BLANCHARD, founder of Blanchard Consulting Group, is a seasoned entrepreneur, consultant, and media producer. He garnered praise for his films *THE ANSWER To Absolutely Everything* and the *FIRESIDE FORUM*. With more than 100,000 client-graduates worldwide, he was elected to the esteemed Transformational Leadership Council. His Ph.D. is from the University of Oregon.

Contact Information

www.rayblanchard.com
youcountnow@gmail.com

Chapter 3

The Scarcity of Abundance

by Traci Williams

*C*onsider that for a minute. As children, we believe that we can do anything, become anyone—the sky's the limit. Have you seen that commercial with kids saying, "When I grow up, I want to be a corporate lackey," or "When I grow up, I want to be a middle manager"? It stands out in our memory because it is so out of place for a child to say or dream something so small. They see the world as a place of abundance.

Here's a great example of that fact. When my daughter was five years old, Haiti was hit with a devastating natural disaster. When we got to school later that week, the Red Cross was collecting donations for them. She was fascinated by the Red Cross and why they would choose to help complete strangers. She saw some news coverage on Haiti and realized the devastation. On that Friday, I picked up my usually happy kindergartner to find her in tears. Her snow globe from Spain had just been crushed under the foot of a fellow student. Both kids were crying. She got in the car and relayed the incident to me and said, "You know what would make me feel better, Mom?" I was waiting for her to say, "ice cream, a movie, another snow globe." Instead, she floored me with this: "I want to give one of my penny banks to the Red Cross for those people in Haiti."

I raced home to find out what time they closed. They were clear across town, and it was Friday rush hour, so we hopped in the car with all four "penny" banks and did our best to deliver directly to their offices. I wanted her to see the people and to tell her story. I had no idea what a difference she would make.

We got to the Red Cross five minutes before closing time. I carried in her arts and crafts "hand-painted" Noah's Ark, a digital pig from the Girl Scouts, another hand-painted pig, and her Hello Kitty penny banks. The director was expecting us and asked for my daughter's name. She replied, "Toni with an 'i'." The director then asked Toni why she was giving this money to the Red Cross. Toni said that she just wanted it to stop. When asked what, she replied, "The pain. I just want all of the pain to stop." They continued to question Toni to find out that this was money she had set aside from doing chores, from collecting change around the house, and from gifts. She was saving this for a trip to Disney World. They asked her if she was sad to be missing Disney World, and she explained that Haiti is a more magical place anyway. "Plus, I can just save more money."

Her entire life savings came to $167.82. She got to pour it into the old-fashioned bank money bags. As we left, some of the people were in tears (including me). Toni's head was held high when she said, "Don't worry. I'll be back. I'm going to start refilling them now."

The director shared this story with the board and on their website. Several people decided to match "Toni with an i's" donation. Later that year, she was recognized by the Red Cross of Austin as a local hero. Imagine the lesson she learned about good deeds and putting others ahead of herself. But also consider our lesson—the lesson for adults. Toni had no reason to believe that she wouldn't make more money or have more money to give. She was coming from a place of abundance.

Even within the limits of the possible, the possibilities are limitless.
—Jules Deeder

As we grow up, we go through some experiences that make us wonder if we'll have enough money to make ends meet, if anyone will ever love us again, if we'll ever get another job . . . you get the idea. Life's experiences can drive into us a sense of scarcity. What do we hear on the news every night? Definitely not a story about a five-year-old giving away her Disney money to people far away from her world. No, we hear about fuel shortages, economic depressions, falling stock prices, scarcity, scarcity, scarcity.

Don't get me wrong. I realize these things happen in life, and that we can become a product of our own experiences, both good and bad. However, your past does not define you. And it definitely does not define your future. Some of us make mistakes and continue to blame or punish ourselves and feel we're not worthy of receiving more or even asking for more. We just settle and feel we deserve it. Or worse. Something awful happens "to" us. We lose a loved one, get a divorce, get fired, lose a home. . . . It's easy to fall into victim mode and to play that card forever so people can pity you. But is that any way to live? You've just placed yourself in scarcity. Maybe not on purpose, but it is where you end up if you choose to "be" a victim.

Awful things happen to everyone. How you respond to them is what makes the difference in how you will live the rest of your life. And the reality is that it is a choice. Your choice.

The fact that the same circumstances will be alike, good and bad,
to different souls proves that the good or bad is not in the circumstances
but only in the mind . . . that encounters it.
—James Allen

Toni woke me up from my own place of scarcity. I had just returned from a convention where we had passed around a water cooler bottle for the Haiti Relief Fund. I had given $50. As a divorced mom starting a fledgling business at the time, I felt generous, as if I deserved a pat on the back. SMACK! Reality check from a five-year-old.

Can you imagine a world where everyone approached life from a childlike place of abundance? I'm not just talking about charities here. I'm talking about abundance of thought, resources, knowledge, love, . . . where there is plenty of everything for everyone. It exists. You just need to take action to see it and to be a part of it.

Abundance versus scarcity rarely has anything to do with the circumstances and everything to do with your own mindset.

When we stop looking at the world as a place that owes us or has taken from us something that we "deserve," we can move into a place where we are free to experience the limitless possibilities available for us to play an active and positive role in the world. There are so many ways to act with an attitude of abundance.

By acting with an abundance mentality, we are often rewarded with abundance. Did Steve Jobs not make a ton of money by making our lives easier, creating jobs, improving technology? Did Warren Buffett not help many people along the way to his fortune? By making that fortune, he's able to help even more people in more ways. Making money is not bad. In fact, making money is great for everyone. And with an attitude of abundance, there's plenty of it out there.

Let me ask you this. Is there not the same amount of money in the world during a depression as there is during a good economy? Yes. It's just in fewer hands. When you think there's not enough, you're basically just saying, "There's not enough for me." It puts you in a victim's mentality and a place of limitations. If Toni had decided there wasn't enough money, would she have given so freely and inspired others to do the same? Abundance can have a trickle effect that can create huge waves of change.

So how do we rewire our brains back to abundance? Action.

As a personal coach, here are a few of my favorite tips I give to clients.

1. **Practice an Attitude of Gratitude**—Take five minutes to start and end your day by being thankful for what you have. Make a list and read through it aloud. For example, instead of stressing over a leaky roof on your house, say out loud that you're thankful to have a home. Sounds different, and more importantly, it makes you feel different.

2. **Say Positive Affirmations**—After you go through your gratitude exercise, read 12 affirmations aloud. Have a balance of physical, financial, spiritual, and intellectual ones. These are not goals. Affirmations should be read as if they are already occurring versus something you want. Here's an example: "Toni loves getting praise from me a minimum of 10 times per day. Her confidence and smile are uplifting. She was so prepared for first grade." Another one could be, "I love being financially free in 2012. It's freed me up to see the Seven Wonders of the World with my partner." You can feel the emotion and be connected with these statements. To learn more about affirmations and how to create them for yourself, I recommend reading Marc Accetta, Tony Robbins, and Eckhart Tolle.

3. **Surround Yourself with Abundant People**—I don't mean "a lot" of people. Look for those people who have the qualities or the life that you've captured in your affirmations. This will give

you daily examples of it working. It takes the ideas or concepts and turns them into reality for you. If you struggle finding these people, then start by reading their books, attending their seminars, or listening to their CDs. Some of my favorites are Robert Kiyosaki, Ayn Rand, Tony Robbins, and Napoleon Hill.

All three of these actions may consume only 30 minutes to one hour of your day, but eventually they will consume your mind. You will feel and act differently toward others and toward yourself. Your inner voice will become your inner coach.

By employing these techniques, I moved from a corporate job, working 60 hours a week and never getting to see my daughter, to following my dreams of entrepreneurship, owning one business and being a partner in another. I can't tell you how different life is for us today. My daughter and I get to travel the world and live richer, fuller lives. I no longer miss events at her school, and I get to choose how I spend my time and my emotions. Are you ready to accept everything life has to offer? The answer is inside of you. You just have to take consistent action to make it your reality. Start now.

Biography

Traci Williams

As a sought-after speaker, consultant, and entrepreneur, TRACI WILLIAMS is the president and CEO of Success You Publishing, Inc. After receiving her masters of education from the University of Texas at Austin, Traci worked with the top executives of a multibillion-dollar corporation to streamline operations and increase revenues, significantly adding to the company's bottom-line profits. After leaving the corporate world, Traci reinvented the learning systems for the #1 most-visited personal development website on the Internet, which led to several hundred thousand dollars a month in added revenues to the company. Today, she runs Success You Publishing while maintaining her own global enterprise helping entrepreneurs create a thriving business in the $8 trillion-a-year travel industry.

Contact Information

www.PartnerWithTraci.com
wayoflifeinfo@gmail.com

Chapter 4

The Money Line

by Marc Accetta

I will never forget the first day I officially became an entrepreneur. I was so excited and filled with optimism. I drove down to the office where I would be conducting my new business, sauntered into my private office, and sat behind the new expensive executive desk I had just purchased to run my empire. I remember how important I felt. It was awesome.

I had a very small staff, since most of the people generating income for me were independent outside sales reps, so it was just me and two other people in the office. But that did not matter, because they worked for me. I was their *boss*.

I spent the next several hours working my butt off. I made several phone calls to my sales reps to motivate them and worked like crazy getting my office organized. I was actually amazed at how fast the day went. Before I knew it, everyone had gone home for the day, and I was still knee-deep in busywork.

The next day was quite similar to the first. In fact, the first several weeks were all quite similar. As my first month of business came to a close, I felt good that I had answered the bell and put in the hours needed to make my new business work. The only problem was that our overall company sales were terrible. Very few of my people were being productive. They were dropping the ball! I was upset with them because I had been wearing out my phone "motivating" them.

I started to get nervous. I had not started my business in a traditional manner. I did not have a business plan. I just thought that I could produce enough sales to justify going out on my own, so I did it. (Side note: That is a bad idea.) Now, I realized that by the first of the next month, I would be short on numerous financial obligations that my new business had generated.

I was panicking and angry with the unproductive people who were not getting the job done. I had set up the office perfectly. It was immaculate. All they had to do was sell the product and everything would have been great. I knew that owning a business could be stressful, but I had not expected this kind of stress so quickly.

At the end of that first month, I had to get a loan from the bank to cover expenses. Truth be told, I had to get a gal I was dating to cosign a loan so I could pay the bills. Something had to change and in a hurry. I was pretty certain this girl would not cosign another loan the following month, and if I even asked her to do so, my possibilities of a long-term romance would be kaput.

I started going back into blame game mode, thinking about everyone who was letting me down, and then it dawned on me that I should make sure I was doing everything I was supposed to be doing before I read them the riot act.

Wow, that was a wake-up call. I started to analyze everything I had accomplished that initial month and realized that even though I had outworked everyone, I had not been productive.

I had logged 10–12 hours each day. I was exhausted, but I was not doing the high income-generating activities I had always done to be successful.

I had thought that since I was now an "entrepreneur," I was a hot shot and didn't need to get my hands dirty. I would simply let "my people" do all the hard work, and I would get all the glory and a lot of the money. I was wrong.

I immediately learned the first lesson of jumping from being an employee to being an owner. The hours you put in are irrelevant! The *only* thing that matters when you are the owner is the results. It doesn't matter how hard you try. It doesn't matter if you hit the numbers you need to hit working 1 hour a day or 20 hours a day. The only thing that matters is hitting your numbers.

That was a radical shift for me. I will now come clean and admit that when I was working for someone else, I sometimes went through the motions and looked like I was doing my job when I was not. But on a job, we trade hours for dollars, so we get paid even if we do not hit the numbers. If you are unproductive on a job long enough, you will eventually get the boot, but it is not an immediate process. It can take months or even years before you pay the price for your lack of productivity.

When you are the owner, the only person you are cheating when you are not productive is yourself. I am fortunate that I looked in the mirror and realized this so early in the game. If I had not, I would have been doomed to failure.

I did not work this way intentionally. I did it because that's the way I had become programmed to work. Most people do not realize that our school systems, while wonderful in many ways, program us to be good employees. By the time we graduate high school (or secondary school), we have spent over 14,000 hours in a classroom. That's a lot of hours.

We all know the story of Pavlov and his dogs, which he trained through classical conditioning to salivate when they heard the bell ring, assuming there would be food there. I don't know exactly how long that programming took, but I would imagine about a week. Imagine how classically conditioned we are after 14,000 hours? That's a lot of weeks!

We learn to show up on time. We learn to be well behaved. We learn to do our work well and in a timely fashion. We learn that others need to be in control and set the schedule and agenda for us, and all we have to do is follow their orders. We get used to being graded and evaluated.

Mostly we learn to watch the clock and put in the hours.

The problem is that we don't know what we don't know. So we aren't usually aware of being programmed to be an employee. To further compound the problem, we don't know where to go to learn how to be a business owner. The truth is, it's uncommon knowledge. And to compound the problem one more time, this programming creates habits in us. We are all creatures of habit, right? And a habit is at least 1,000 times more powerful than our willpower. Therefore, breaking our conditioning and creating the new right habits is a real challenge.

Most employees have a "What do I need to do" mentality. They wait for their boss to tell them what is expected of them, and then they normally do that much and no more. That mindset will kill an entrepreneur.

So with that information now in hand, I went back to work. The difference was that now I was not getting organized, or calling others to motivate them; now I started doing the highest income-generating activities I knew how to do. The results were immediate and dramatic.

I had always been a very good sales person. That was why I started my own business. So I went back to mission number one: acquiring new customers.

By the end of the month, I had generated enough revenue to pay all the bills and have a few bucks left over for myself. Not only that, my girlfriend was ecstatic.

So let me ask you a few questions:

- Have you been confusing working hours with focusing on results?
- Are you teachable and willing to learn how to break your old habits and to think and act like a business owner?
- Do you know what you highest income-generating activities are?

Almost every new entrepreneur admits feeling that putting in long hours is enough to get the job done. But it's not the number of hours that matters—it's how you use them.

You *have to be teachable* to make it. You need to embrace the concept of being a lifelong learner. I have read hundreds of books on success and business principles since I started my first business. I have attended well over 100 live seminars too, easily eclipsing what I spent on my college education.

The last question is the big one, though. If you have not identified what your top income-generating activities are, you will most likely not spend your prime business hours doing them.

At my live seminars, with my personal coaching clients, and on some of my advanced webinar series, I teach the concept of the Money Line. It's simple yet very effective. First, identify what your prime income-generating hours are. If you are not sure, let me give you an example of what I mean.

My first job was in home sales. Virtually all my sales calls were on weekdays from 6 p.m. to 9 p.m., and on Saturday afternoons. How ridiculous would it have been if I did *anything* other than sales presentations during those critical income-generating hours?

I had many other things to do. I had to do paperwork. I had to make phone calls to set up the sales appointments. I had to train new sales reps.

Before I knew the Money Line system, I would do those things whenever I wanted to. Once I learned how to maximize my peak income-earning hours, I only did those things *outside* my prime earning hours!

An attorney who owns his own firm attended a couple of my live events. He ended up retaining me to do some personal coaching with him. The first thing I did was have him make a list of all the duties he needs to do in any given week at his firm. Then we determined his peak income-generating hours.

Next, we decided what his highest income-generating activities were. We quickly determined that he was delegating these to one of his employees because he was *too busy* to do them himself.

So I had him go to his list and determine which things he had to *do* himself. Then we determined what things he could *delegate* to someone else, and finally we determined if there was anything he could altogether *ditch*.

With one simple adjustment, his business totally changed. He delegated the tasks that were preventing him from doing his highest-income-generating activity and started doing that work himself, and he was free to do it throughout all his peak earning hours.

For him, that work was doing the initial interview with a prospective client, which ultimately determined if they would retain him and become a paying client. His business went up about 400% the first year after he made that simple change.

Would you like to have your business grow by 400% this year?

Grab a piece of paper and draw a line down the left side from the top of the page to the bottom. That is your Money Line. Then draw three more identical lines (each about two inches to the right of the one before it).

Now list all your work activities down the left side of the Money Line. Once you have done that, then determine which ones you have to *do*, which you can *delegate*, and which you can *ditch*. Next, take all the ones that you have to do yourself and put them in either column 2 (must be done during peak hours), column 3 (important to do in peak hours, but not your highest priority), column 4 (would be nice to do ASAP, but not during peak hours), or column 5 (could be done whenever).

Then prioritize doing everything that is in column 2 (right on the money line) during your peak hours. If you have extra time, go on to the 3s, and then the 4s, and so on.

I know this may seem elementary, but once you master this concept, you are well on your way to dramatically increasing productivity.

Do peak earning activities during peak earning hours and maximize the Money Line!

Biography

Marc Accetta

MARC ACCETTA has owned five successful businesses over the last 20 years, including his primary company, MarcAccettaSeminars. He has trained a million people all over the world in his live events. Marc has served on the board for his local Big Brothers Big Sisters for the last five years and is the director of training for WorldVentures.

Contact Information

MarcAccetta.com
ThePowerOfOneShow.com
Facebook.com/MarcAcetta
Info@marcaccetta.com
972-381-8675

Chapter 5

The Psychology of Winning

by Johnny Wimbrey

Winning isn't everything, but wanting to win is.
—Vince Lombardi

Success leaves clues. There are no coincidences to winning. No one wins by chance or luck. Winners win because they want to win. Winners think about winning all the time. Best-selling recording artist Nelly released an international hit entitled "What Does It Take to Be Number One?" The chorus line says number "two is not a winner and three nobody remembers." This album went straight to the top of the charts and made Nelly an international phenomenon. He wrote the song before he became number one in the public's eyes, yet he understood the concept of winning and attitude. Winners eat, sleep, and breathe the concept of victory—of being number one. If you want to be in first place, you first must see yourself there. You must sell yourself on the fact that you are a winner and that you are number one, long before it's obvious to others. "Faith is the substance of things hoped for and the evidence of things not seen." You must think like a winner to become one.

Terry L. Hornbuckle authored a book titled *See Your Future, Be Your Future*. In this book he talks about how important—and how necessary—it is for you to see your future in order for your hopes, aspirations, and goals to become a manifested reality. You must believe without a shadow of a doubt that you deserve to win. And you must practice seeing yourself as the winner to be a winner.

> *Only a man who knows what it is like to be defeated*
> *can reach down to the bottom of his soul and come up with an extra*
> *ounce of power it takes to win when the match is even.*
> —Muhammad Ali

Voted *USA Today's* Athlete of the Century, heavyweight champion Muhammad Ali mastered the psychology of winning. Long before Ali was the greatest fighter of all time, he told the world he was the greatest. Long before the world knew who he was, he told the local gyms that he was the greatest. And long before he became confident enough to become outspoken, he told himself he was the greatest. Ali first convinced himself that he was the greatest before he could convince anyone else. What's more important to remember than any of the above is this: Not only is it necessary for you to continually remind yourself that you are a winner, it is mandatory for your opponent to see, hear, and feel your confidence in your own abilities to win. When your opponent begins to imagine you winning, half the battle is already won.

> *Other people's opinion of you does not have to become your reality.*
> —Les Brown

Who is your opponent? Like your foe, your opponent can be anything or anyone who tries to keep you from coming out of the box.

My opponents are the odds that stand against me. Society and statistics tell us that because I'm biracial, was born in the projects, lived on welfare, had an alcoholic for a father, and came from a single-parent home that I supposedly will never have any control of what ultimately will determine my future. According to society, I was supposed to have suffered emotionally at the hands of my peers because of my undetermined race; I am supposed to be struggling with alcoholic tendencies; I'm supposed to be socially and economically depressed; and my ever experiencing a successful marriage is not likely to happen.

But my reality is very different. I could have had problems in school about my race, but it was obvious that I was confident and very satisfied with who I was. In high school I ended up being Homecoming King, Most Likely to Be Remembered, and Class Favorite. I don't have any dependency on alcohol, I live a very nice lifestyle, and my wife and I have been married happily for over five years and are still best friends today.

Listen very closely. Never let others' experiences become your reality! You are the only one who can officially determine who and what you will become. If you see yourself in society's box, that's where you will be. Never let anyone create your world for you, because they will always create it too small.

Am I a freak of nature? No! I am simply programmed by God to be the head and not the tail, to be above and not beneath anyone or anything. I was designed to win, and so I choose to walk with my footsteps toward my God-given right. I am mentally programmed to win. I am a record breaker! I am confident and not arrogant.

Everyone experiences hard times and struggles, but all winners have one thing in common—we don't like to lose. Society has programmed us to think that if you're having trouble in your marriage, get a divorce. Almost all situations have an easy way out, but the prize for the race is not always given to the quick; instead, it is given to the one who perseveres and finishes the race. Winners understand that through the thick and thin, we must win. Failure is not an option for winners. They say winners never quit. I can guarantee you a quitter will never be a winner.

A true winner also understands the importance of surrounding himself or herself with other winners. I have made it a personal goal in my life to constantly introduce myself to—and continuously surround myself with—people who stretch me. All winners understand that you must get out of your comfort zone. You can't learn how to swim in shallow waters. Don't be afraid of the deep. It's hard to move to a higher level if everyone around you is beneath you or on the same level as you. I don't mean beneath you as in you are better as a person than they are, because we know that we are *all* created equally. What I mean is, for example, if you want to become an executive at your job, then you need to expose yourself to the mentality of an executive. There are a lot of people who are, or have been, where you are trying to go. You cannot follow a parked car. Hang around winners and you will become a winner too!

The Importance of Having Mentors

Winners understand and value the importance of having mentors. I have found that in many cases, people use the word "mentor" very loosely. A mentor, first of all, is someone you know personally. You may admire someone on TV, but he or she is not your mentor unless you have access to that person. You choose your mentor; your mentor does not choose you. You may be approached by someone who wants to put you under his or her wing and guide you, but until you choose to go, this person is not your mentor. In addition, your mentor must accept the role, or he or she is not a mentor. A mentor should be able to correct you on the spot; you submit immediately and take heed of his or her direction. This is why you choose your mentor. Because the moment you begin to unwillingly receive advice, correction, or even open rebuke, then that person is no longer your mentor.

Synonyms for the word *mentor*: teacher, adviser, tutor, counselor, guru, guide. Webster's dictionary defines the mentor as "A trusted counselor or guide."

In order to have a mentor, you must be a protégé!

Synonyms and definition of the word *protégé*: dependent, student, disciple, one who accepts the charge. You can have different mentors for different areas of your life. For example, you may have a physical mentor, a spiritual mentor, and a financial mentor. It's great if all of these are the same person, but it's not necessary.

How Do You Choose a Mentor?

Your mentor should

1. have something that you would also like to have or experience. Example: You play the saxophone and he or she is very good with the sax.

2. agree to mentor you.

3. be someone who can tell you *no!*

4. have a lifestyle you respect in every facet.

5. be someone you can be honest with, no matter what!

> *In the multitude of counselors there is safety.*
> —King Solomon

Mentors' jobs are to protect us. That's why it's very important that we be open and honest with them so they can tell, show, and give us everything we need that is in our best interests. True mentors will tell us what we need to hear, instead of what we want to hear. Great mentors will inspect what they expect. In other words, they won't just tell us what to do; they will follow up or make sure we report our results. Mentors are not dictators but advisers who want us to succeed without sacrificing our integrity. Great mentors will never ask us to compromise good character to get to the top.

A great financial mentor will show you how to master your money, instead of your money mastering you. When your money tells you what to do, you are in trouble, but when you can tell your money what to do, you can and will experience true wealth.

I once read that open rebuke is better than hidden love. A great mentor understands that he or she must tell it to you like it is.

A winner is also a great protégé, who will apply the mentor's advice. A mentor has every right to terminate a relationship with a rebellious protégé. Likewise, the protégé has every right to terminate a relationship with his or her mentor. Keep in mind, if you find yourself jumping from mentor to mentor because they are not what you expected them to be, chances are they are not the ones with the problems.

I will tell you from experience that I have gotten my feelings hurt by my mentors plenty of times, but remember, I chose them. Winners are not afraid of constructive criticism and understand that it takes iron to sharpen iron.

My wife, Crystal, and I are very blessed to have incredible marital mentors, Eben and Sara Conner, who hold us accountable to each other. We chose them; they did not choose us. They have counseled us on several occasions. I must admit that when I know I am right, I am very quick to call them to referee when Crystal and I are having intense fellowships (arguments). I do confess that most the time, I call them in so Crystal can get help (because I am right). Usually, I end up being the one getting the most help.

Did you know that it is possible to deceive yourself? Deception would not be deception if it were obvious! You can be off track and not know it. And without correct navigation, you will eventually crash.

Crystal and I know that Eben and Sara want us to win in every facet of our lives. And since they have our best interests at heart, we agree to submit to their wisdom. Wisdom is the application of knowledge. So when they share their knowledge, as their protégés, we must apply their instructions, regardless of who is at fault. A winner knows when to swallow his or her pride to resolve a higher cause or purpose. Winners understand that it is impossible to win by themselves.

Winners Must Win!

Winners don't see success as an option; we see it as something that we must have. Average people want to win, but winners must win. While the majority of the world is talking about what they want to happen, the mentality of the winner is focused on what must happen. As a winner, you must be able to convert every one of your wants to your musts. When you want something, it's optional. But when you must have something, it's non-negotiable. Everyone wants to be successful; only a very few *must* be successful.

So how do you turn your wants into your musts? I've done seminars across the nation on this topic. And when I ask the audience to give me a list of things that are a must in their lives, here are some of the common answers that I get.

Things People Must Do:

- be at work on time
- pay bills on time
- eat

- bathe

- buy groceries

- pay taxes

Here is a common list of answers that I get when I ask for things they want.

Things People Want To Do:

- eat healthy

- exercise

- go on vacation

- pray every day

- give to charity

- spend more time with family

Okay, by now you should get the point. The only difference between the things that you must have or do and the things that you want to have or do is you. Your attitude determines your ability to succeed.

Typically, the things that most people see as a must are tied to negative consequences. For example, if you don't eat, you starve. Or if you don't show up for work on time, you will get fired. In other words, most people are programmed to perform to prevent immediate negative reactions. You have a why for all your musts.

Few are driven by the thrill of success. Those who are understand that they must do today what others don't, to have tomorrow what others won't. These are the ones who have the ability to make things happen, and who are self-disciplined. It is very important to have a reason, or a why, for everything that you want.

Example:

I *must* be successful because I *want* to leave an inheritance for my children's children.

When you find your why in everything that you want and become passionate with a burning desire for the end result, your wants will become musts. Therefore, you must find your why for all of your wants.

Wants + Whys = Musts

- I *must* eat healthy to live longer.
- I *must* exercise for energy and for good health.
- I *must* go on vacation because I work hard.
- I *must* pray every day to stay spiritually strong.
- I *must* give to charity to save lives.
- I *must* spend more time with my family to show my love.

My cause is bigger than me, and because my wants have whys that are much more important than selfish desires, I am willing to fight for the end result. You must be willing to fight for the cause of your wants. It's hard to fight for something without a cause, so connect all your wants to all your whys so that all your dreams will come to fruition.

Biography

Johnny Wimbrey

Internationally acclaimed talk show host, author, and motivational-speaking giant JOHNNY WIMBREY lives by one rule: Don't let your past determine your future. Living a real-life "G to Gent" story, Wimbrey continues to inspire and change the lives of corporate execs and inner city kids alike.

Contact Information

johnnywimbrey.com

Chapter 6

Lead Yourself and the Rest Will Follow

by Juan Ramon Garcia

You must take personal responsibility. You cannot change the circumstances, the seasons, or the wind, but you can change yourself. That is something you have charge of.
—Jim Rohn

Taking 100% responsibility for your life is the secret to being successful, no matter who you are, what has happened in your life, or what you've done (or not done). All of it. The good, the bad, the actions you may regret, and the actions you take in response to or regardless of what others do.

Only when you remove excuses and blame from your mind and focus on your infinite possibilities can you take actions today that result in realizing your dreams tomorrow. If you don't control your present (or don't believe you are in control), you put your future in the hands of others—and dreams held in others' hands will always be out of your reach.

My success in sales comes from leading myself first and believing in myself. Time and again, I am asked to turn around a company or a sales region with poor sales numbers. I have done this in different cultures, countries, and companies, in the United States, Mexico, and South and Central America in Ecuador, Guatemala, Paraguay, Uruguay, Colombia, Chile, Argentina. . . .

When I arrive to manage new multicultural teams, I often have to prove myself and lead by example. I have to believe in myself. I do not tell my team how to increase sales—I show them. I overachieve my goals, the sales team sees how I do it (and more important, sees that it's possible), and they follow my lead. When I leave, I leave successful companies that go from few clients to several, regions that go from last to first in sales.

Most critical of all, I leave sales teams able to carry on this success without me. That is the ultimate goal of leadership. To be willing to go it alone and lead by example in the beginning so that in the end, everyone succeeds together.

I am not trying to make myself sound great. I'm telling you all this because I am absolutely no different from you. What exactly do I do to lead myself and others to success? I follow seven basic steps in my everyday life to achieve—and often exceed—my goals.

Seven Steps to Success

Sooner or later, those who win are those who think they can.
—Robert Bach

1. Activate your intentions and passions.

I start each day reminding myself of what I want to accomplish, keeping my passion alive for everything I do. That excitement you feel when you're starting something new? Bring that to everything you do and you will not only motivate yourself to accomplish your goals, you will experience the everyday happiness and drive necessary to keep going no matter how rough the tasks ahead.

Optimism is key to keeping that passion alive, going into your day confident that you will succeed in achieving your goals. The beauty of optimism and confidence is that they are self-fulfilling. The more optimism you have about your success, the more success you experience, which gives you evidence that you have reason to be optimistic and confident about your success.

2. Set attainable goals.

Dream big, but achieve your dream with attainable goals along the way. This gives you the satisfaction and reward of accomplishment every day, which motivates you to keep going.

Setting realistic goals means realizing you can make it to the moon but you can't walk on the sun. It also means the opposite: not ruling out as unattainable a goal you've only approached in one or two ways.

For example, a salesman on my team told me that a potential buyer wasn't interested in selling our product in his stores. The buyer said similar products hadn't moved, and the salesman didn't see any way to enroll him. This buyer required a different approach.

I asked him to give me one store. If I couldn't sell the product in that one store, I would be 100 percent responsible. I would buy the unsold product personally. Just give me that one opportunity to prove myself. He agreed. Now the product is carried in all 13 of his stores.

When evaluating whether a goal is attainable, don't rule something out unless you're sure you've tried every angle. If you've gone in from the left, try the right. If that doesn't work, come in from above. If that doesn't work, approach from behind. Try, try, and try.

Challenge yourself to stretch what you're capable of and challenge the people you lead to do the same.

3. Analyze and evaluate your goals.

Your goals should be part of a clear strategy that takes into account all possible obstacles and how you will overcome them. Your goals should also be as informed as possible. Do your homework: market research, business reviews, budgets, P&L, team building.

Have a clear system in place to measure performance. If you are selling a product, you should have a clear idea of inventory, numbers sold, what brand is selling. Make your goals quantifiable so that you can determine easily whether you met them, and if not, why. Low motivation? Lack of belief in the product? A type of buyer who requires a different approach? Too much focus on selling the product or service and not enough focus on selling the brand?

When you are able to pinpoint exactly what is going wrong, you can approach the problem with honesty. Use candor when addressing the people you lead. Don't be afraid of telling them the truth about what's not working and why. The only way to act on a solution is if everyone clearly understands the problem in the first place.

When you are not getting the results you want, change what you are doing. If your life is not what you want it to be, evaluate what exactly is going wrong and come up with a different strategy.

When facing a problem, look to yourself, not to external circumstances or people. What can *you* do differently? Yes, this applies even when the problem is a particular team member's performance. You won't be successful by just throwing up your hands and blaming him. What can *you* do to help him improve? Are you asking him to do something that you are not willing to do? Does he believe in what he's doing? Does he believe in himself? Do you? It always comes back to you.

4. Focus.

One of the main reasons we don't get where we want to be in life is lack of focus. It's easy to get swept up in everyday problems, to go from putting out one fire to another, and to start acting randomly to achieve what we want instead of reminding ourselves of our personal and professional objectives and how exactly we want to achieve them.

Keep your focus on possibilities and on your intentions, not on your current or past resentments. Be present in the moment, in what you are doing now to achieve your dreams. Do what you need to do to reconnect with your mission.

This might mean renewing your passion. It might mean reconnecting with others and reminding yourself that you are a team. You might need to reconnect with yourself and your emotions, especially if you are getting in your own way when trying to stay focused on your goals.

5. Remain committed.

Many of us see mistakes and failures as character flaws. However, they are just a part of life, a part of being human. The only true failure is giving up.

Some people dwell on their mistakes to the point of losing the confidence to keep going. Others try to devalue or forget their past, but they lose the lessons they can gain from mistakes. Either way, the past becomes an excuse for not committing to success.

I have made major mistakes in my life. Most of us have. I know how easy it is to slip back into self-destructive habits, procrastination, excuses. I know what it feels like to have no car, no clothes, no money, no home, simply broken—and I know that blaming others or my circumstances did not change my situation. Taking responsibility for my life did. I will always remember where I came from and where I could go back to if I lose my commitment.

My faith in God and my faith in myself help me to see mistakes as ways to strengthen my commitment. Mistakes mean I've learned something that will help me get where I'm going. Pursuing a dream I believe in also helps me to stay focused on the outcome rather than on the often tedious processes involved in accomplishing goals.

Which brings me back to passion. If you are not passionate about your dreams, about what you are doing, you will have a tough time staying committed. Money doesn't keep you motivated in the long run if you don't enjoy and believe in what you're doing to earn it. If you are having trouble staying committed, ask yourself, are you truly passionate about what you're doing?

Commitment to success comes back to taking responsibility for yourself but also for those who work for and with you. In addition to being a manager, I am a public speaker, a trainer, and a mentor for the people who work for me. I am responsible for not only hiring the right people for the job but also training them to excel. I train myself to be knowledgeable in the products, including the culture of those products, so that I can train everyone else in the same—including my clients.

Taking that extra step to educate your clients about your products makes an enormous difference in their commitment to selling those products to their customers and to continue buying them for themselves.

In the end, success is not about me. It is about the people I am working with as well, the other salespeople, the distributor, the client. If even one team member were different, the results would be different. Your success is a result of everyone's work and commitment.

6. Talk to a mentor

Having someone to talk to when doubt takes over is essential in remaining focused, committed, and confident when pursuing your goals and dreams. Spiritual, personal, and professional mentors you admire will open your heart, soul, and mind, and help you see from new perspectives. Often, we get stuck in a narrow way of looking at something. A mentor widens your view of possibilities.

Choose people who have been through similar battles and can understand where you're coming from. Choose people who model success the way you define success for yourself. Three of my mentors have been Matt Morris, Ray Blanchard, and Jack Welch.

7. Execute everything you set for yourself.

You are where you are now because
of actions you have taken in the past.

Obviously, you won't be successful if you don't follow through on your objectives. Execution is a set of behaviors, a technique. You and everyone you lead must have the discipline to execute so that you have the competitive advantage.

Steps 1 through 6 help me ensure that every company I lead has this advantage. I start with the optimism and passion I need to motivate me. I set goals that I can attain but that also stretch what I'm capable of. I put a clear strategy in place that helps me surmount obstacles and measure performance—mine and others'—so that we can adapt what we're doing if it's not working. I do whatever I need to do to stay focused and committed and to lead others to do the same. When necessary, this includes talking to a mentor to renew my sense of purpose and confidence.

Of course, the more I follow through, the more I enjoy my accomplishments, which motivates me to continue following through. In other words, the more successful you are through your own actions, the easier it is to continue to be successful, to maintain the confidence you need to achieve your dreams. You are where you are now because of actions you have taken in the past. The results of your actions today will determine where you are tomorrow. Results do not lie.

Whether you are selling a product, a service, or yourself as an entrepreneur—leading hundreds, twenty, or one—you have the power to create the life you've always wanted. Don't wait for circumstances to change, or for other people to act. Take the lead. Success will follow.

You have to believe in yourself when no one else does.
That's what makes you a winner.
—Venus Williams

Biography
Juan Ramon Garcia

JUAN RAMON GARCIA is a top-performing sales and promotion professional, public speaker, and trainer, with award-winning excellence in exceeding sales quotas; managing, training, and supporting teams; and driving regional growth and profitability. He has worked throughout the United States, from California to New York, and Mexico as well as in South and Central America for companies such as Malher (a Nestle company), Klass Time, Ltd., Michel, and Deloitte & Touche (formerly Arthur Andersen). He is in high demand as a speaker and sales professional because of his reputation for going above and beyond expectations and encouraging his team to do the same.

Born in Mexico City and raised in Guadalajara, at 16, Garcia attended Valley Forge Military Academy in Wayne, Pennsylvania, where he gained a strong sense of discipline and self-respect that would stay with him throughout his exceptionally successful sales and management career. He majored in international business from the "Harvard of Mexico," Instituto Tecnológico y de Estudios Superiores de Monterrey (TEC of Monterrey).

Contact Information

www.facebook.com/garciajuanramon
www.twitter.com/garciajuanramon
committedandaccountable.blogspot.com/
garciajuanramon@hotmail.com

Chapter 7

25 Birthday Cakes

by Blake Fleischacker

s I sit here and type, I realize that I have lived a longer life than some, but a shorter life than most. Ornaments have hung from 25 Christmas trees. Candles have flickered on top of 25 birthday cakes. I have lived one quarter of a century, and I have spent it looking up. I think that is the byproduct of being the youngest of three children, as well as being raised by eternal optimists. Negativity was not allowed in the house, even if he took his shoes off at the door. Aside from hiding vegetables under the placemat and in the dog's mouth, I spent my dinners listening to Dad's sermons on the value of manual labor and manners while Mom programmed us to be thankful for one thing every day. I am fascinated by how much I have grown to appreciate the fundamentals that were discussed at the dinner table.

Birthday Cakes 0–14

My Velcro shoes walked me to elementary school until I learned the power of shoelaces. My Ninja Turtles backpack usually contained a few items of homework and a packed lunch. For a while, I was cute. My freckles drew in the ladies when I was a young boy, but they soon faded into the most severe case of acne the local dermatologist had ever seen. Entering my teens with a research-worthy dose of acne taught me the cold reality of having a visible stigma. Classmates came to know me for my face rather than my friendship. Heavy medications were taking a toll on my body. Weekly facial injections were taking a toll on my spirit. Little did I know that success insights were at the ends of the fingers pointing out my damaged skin.

In a technology-based world, where we can work from home and type to talk, it becomes difficult to walk a mile in someone else's shoes. I was grateful when people would try seeing life through my eyes. It reminded me that I was welcome, I was human, and I was still entitled to success. As a result, I now surround myself with people who work hard to account for the other side of every story. If cut off on the highway, most people grow angry and make it known. A select few remind themselves that there may be good intentions behind that person's actions and important details that are missing in the scenario. Someone may be rushing to his wife who is going into labor. Someone may be running out of time to visit her dying child. Success means taking the time to exercise empathy. In doing so, you will learn more about yourself and others.

Birthday Cakes 15–18 (Summer)

My white dress shirt, Snoopy tie, and black apron were the uniform customers saw as I stood behind the checkout packing groceries. My first summer job was as a grocery clerk at the local store by my cottage. My reference points for success were a fully loaded section of soda, a long row of shopping carts, and a bag packed with the eggs and bread on top. Looking back, I did not even realize the true value I was bringing to the customers. I knew that the cans needed to be stocked with the labels facing out. I knew that the carts were to be collected every 30 minutes. I did not appreciate the big picture back then, but I do now. I worry that many of us fail to appreciate the greater power of the work people do in this life. Grocery clerks do not stock shelves, they feed families. Emergency telephone operators do not receive calls, they save lives. Taxi drivers do not just drive, they enable people to perform in their daily lives. I define successful people as those who go out of their way to remind individuals of their true significance in this world. Let people know what would not be possible without them. Go out of your way to deliver a thoughtful, meaningful thank-you for the work that people do.

Birthday Cakes 15–18

My hand clenched the handle on my trumpet case as I entered the high school doors. School band was one of my passions during my life between the lockers. Without passion, it is practically impossible to achieve success. My involvement in the arts earned me more ridicule than respect. Excited to make music, I accepted the ridicule and trusted that respect was around the corner. I was right. Deciding to pursue my passions granted me entrance into greater circles of opportunity. I dove into student leadership and was able to be on a team that affected the success of the entire school community. I connected with teachers and learned their secrets to success. Eventually, people realized my commitment and respected my decision to be comfortable in my own skin.

"You can never make the right decision. You can only make decisions, and then make them right." I heard that quote from my dad, and he likely heard it from someone else. Regardless of its source, the quote is my favorite mantra. It helped with the daily decisions of high school and all the decisions that followed. Success is built on a series of wise decisions, and I am overjoyed that I decided to follow passion rather than punks. Music was my way of showing my personality, and my personality helped me deliver the speech as the student-elected valedictorian. By the end of high school I had learned the power of always showing your personality, because you never know who may be watching.

Birthday Cakes 18–25

My Buzz Lightyear bedsheets were a definite conversation piece in my university residence room. I could list the common lessons that people can lift from their postsecondary textbooks, but my foundations for life and leadership got laid in residence. My student and then professional life in residence combined to a total of seven years and 6,000 roommates. I was passionate about the community spirit in residence, so I decided to stay involved. As soon as I graduated, I was hired to be a residence manager.

In a world that becomes even more of a melting pot, I can say that I was privileged to learn what life is like being neighbor to a collection of cultures. Developing relationships made university fun, but developing community made university meaningful. Students moved in at the start of each year as strangers, and I had the opportunity to help them connect like family. I was a member of a team of people that worked to serve the needs of young adults.

We saw the good, and we saw the bad. We saw the happy, and we saw the sad. Success was found in the student who overcame homesickness. Success was found in the roommate relationship that was getting repaired. Success was found when a student considered giving up on life and we connected him to resources to get back on track. Residence life exposed me to the intricacies of human life. I grew to understand that humans share more similarities than differences. We all have a story, and it is developed in that space between our arrival and our exit on this earth. I learned that successful relationships require hard work and that successful communities require even harder work.

All the Other Birthday Cakes

As a 25-year-old, I have spent more of my life at my parents' dinner table than at my own. The dinner conversations sent me successfully through my first 25 years of life. As eternal optimists, Mom and Dad's commitment to the bright side is what enabled me to draw the value of empathy out of the struggle of acne. The routine manual labor is what taught me the value of hard work and the bigger picture behind stocking shelves and collecting carts. Eliminating negativity is why I was drawn to the positive experiences derived from my passions in high school. Saying thank you is what kept me invested in residence life.

Leaving home, I decided to make my parents proud and thank everyone who made a positive impact on me during university. When you appreciate the world around you, opportunities begin to present themselves. That is why I stayed. My parents are my role models for success. The most important thing I have learned about success is from them: Say thank you to the people who have made you successful along the way. Bob and Judy Fleischacker, consider this my thank-you. You have helped me lay the foundation for my next 25 years, and I guarantee I will commit it to paper. Perhaps I will begin next week, when I blow out the candles on my 26th birthday cake.

Biography

Blake Fleischacker

BLAKE FLEISCHACKER lived and worked with over 6,000 students as a residence manager at the University of Western Ontario. Having spoken to over 10,000 students and professionals, Blake is a highly sought-after trainer and keynote speaker, and the author of "Campus Gets Wasted." Blake is blessed to have an outstanding family and girlfriend who inspire him to write.

Contact Information

www.blakefly.com
blake@blakefly.com
1-877-987-4359

Chapter 8

Don't Just Achieve Success—Live It

by Aaron Byerlee

I grew up on a farm in South Australia. Our nearest neighbor was about 10 kilometers away, and the nearest town was 30. It was an isolated place to grow up, but fun for a young adventurous lad.

My parents have always been great role models for me. As the oldest of five, I learned a hard work ethic, a good attitude, morals, integrity, honesty—and, being on a farm, how to eat quickly! Although as a youngster I didn't know what an entrepreneur was—and certainly didn't know how to spell it—I was born with the drive to be as successful as possible in whatever I did.

When I was only 5 years old, I set up a "shop," selling my toys back to my parents or to my brothers and sisters. As I got older, I developed more advanced money-making ideas (some involving chickens, but that's a long story).

Most of you have the same drive to be successful or you wouldn't be reading this book. What you do with that drive, however, can leave you stuck in park, spinning your wheels, or accelerating toward every destination you dream of.

I now enjoy a dream lifestyle in Sydney, Australia, with my beautiful partner Nicole. I work from home when I want and travel all over the world, helping others to live their dreams. I am in line with my priorities and passions—I am having fun and I have choice, a lifestyle I love, good relationships, and freedom.

How did I do it? By applying 10 principles of success to everything I do.

1. Have a dream that excites *and* scares you, and adapt the right mindset to achieve it. Devour as many audios and books as possible on personal development.

2. Have a BURNING desire to make it happen. Desire alone will not be strong enough to get you there. Everyone has desire.

3. Take MASSIVE action. Action alone will not get you there.

4. Surround yourself with people, including mentors, who will inspire your success.

5. Become an expert at something. Reading five books on a topic will give you more knowledge on that topic than 95% of people.

6. Set your goals. Not realistic ones—ultimate ones. Write them down, read them out loud twice a day as if you have already achieved them. Record them on your mp3 player and listen to them daily.

7. Believe in yourself and what you are doing 100%.

8. Lead by example. People will do what you do, not what you say.

9. Take responsibility. It is your fault and your fault alone if you are or are not successful.

10. Be persistent. Never give up, no matter what.

Dream, Desire, and Act

When I was 22, I wanted to be rich and successful. I wanted to retire young, with residual income. My dream excited and scared me, but I had yet to develop the right mindset to achieve it.

Then I read *Rich Dad, Poor Dad,* by Robert Kiyosaki. Within two weeks, I sold my pride and joy car—a $30,000 Berlina Commodore—and bought a cheap (and way less attractive to the opposite sex) $3,000 Honda Civic. Why? Because Robert Kiyosaki says that cars are a money pit, and I should buy only appreciating assets. So I followed his advice. I wasn't mucking around.

A few months after that, I bought my first business—a gym. Why? Because Robert Kiyosaki says that to be rich, I had to "mind my own business," meaning that 80% of financially free people owned their own businesses. So that's what I did.

At 22, that car was everything to me. But I knew I couldn't wait around until I saved enough money to buy my own business. That would have been taking action, and I wouldn't be where I am today if my burning desire to be successful hadn't led me to take *massive* action.

Surround Yourself with Success

The gym was great for a young guy with big aspirations because I got to train successful business owners and entrepreneurs, including Sean Disbury from Gotta Getta Group and Phil Hoffmann from Phil Hoffmann Travel. Both were big influences and a great help for me during this time. Needless to say, these guys got some boring treadmill sessions while I drilled them on every aspect of marketing, business, and success. I was learning the importance of surrounding myself with successful people, especially mentors who were successful doing what I wanted to do.

When you look for a mentor or coach, be sure to find someone who has successfully done what you want to do *in the way that you want to do it.* You wouldn't hire a financial adviser who has to ride the bus to work. If you want residual income, don't choose a mentor who's rich but works 80 hours a week.

Surrounding yourself with success also means avoiding "pullers"— people who don't want you to succeed, who are negative, closed minded, and jealous. They want to pull you back down to be with them. How you deal with pullers will determine your level of success.

Look at the five people you hang around with most. Your success is very close to theirs, right? If you want to see your success go to a new level, hang out with people who are more successful than you and watch what happens.

Become an Expert

Being successful means constantly learning. Brad Sugars' seminars and books taught me what real-life marketing was all about. His teachings on business and marketing were one of the main reasons I transformed a five-year-old struggling gym into one of the top two performing businesses in our group.

But the gym was just a step toward my larger dream of success. I wanted to be a millionaire by age 30. So I learned all I could about property investment. Four weeks after reading Steve McKnight's *From 0 to 130 Properties in 3.5 Years,* I bought my first property for just $80,000. I sold it a year later for $160,000 and was officially in love with real estate. Around this time, I also sold my first gym for a tidy profit, moved to Sydney, Australia, bought two more gyms and seven more properties.

Just remember: You can read all the books and attend all the seminars you want and feel like you are doing something, but until you take *massive action*, nothing will happen for you. These principles for success only work when you apply all of them to your life.

Set Ultimate Goals

At 28 my priorities had started to change. Success and money at whatever cost no longer made sense. I was tired of working 80+ hour weeks, dealing with staff, risk, overheads, and stress.

I had learned that what we really want when we dream is often much bigger than we recognize. My dream to be wealthy had less to do with my bank account than with what that money would allow me to do—to have the lifestyle I wanted, to have fun, freedom, choice, and the time to build and enjoy good relationships.

Getting rich had become a realistic goal for me. But having the *lifestyle* I wanted was the ultimate goal. To get there I decided I would need to master the Internet.

The Internet is the single most powerful tool to generate residual income. But there was one problem—I had no computer skills whatsoever. I could send an e-mail (as long as it did not have an attachment), and I could Google something. That was literally it. But I was determined to be successful online just as I had been in my other businesses.

I wrote down and recorded my new goals as if I had already achieved them. I read and listened to them daily to program my subconscious mind for success. The subconscious doesn't know the difference between what's true or not. Tell your subconscious you are successful, and you will believe it and make it happen.

Just be sure your ultimate goals are clear. If you dream of buying a big house, imagine every detail of that house. If you dream of having a different lifestyle, imagine every detail of your perfect day. Envision how your ultimate goals fit into the bigger picture of your dreams to motivate you to keep pursuing them.

You will always do whatever you want to do based on your priorities. Always. We all live by a set of priorities or values whether we know it or not. You will always do and ultimately become what you think about the most.

Dream, Desire, Act—Repeat

The principles of success aren't a checklist that you complete and then you're done. They are a way of living successfully. With each dream or goal fulfilled, celebrate your success—then set the bar higher. Develop the burning desire for your new dreams and goals, then take massive action. Success is a cycle that widens what you're capable of with each new dream you aspire to.

Pursuing my new goals required becoming an expert again. I teamed up with my good friend and fellow gym owner Craig Schulze to learn about and start an online empire. Craig had about the same Internet and computer skills as I did, so the learning and fun began.

Over the next three years, we paid a small fortune for mentors, seminars, workshops, and websites, not to mention the cost of trial and error. Great mentors for me through this time were legends such as Matt Morris, who inspired me to sell my physical business, burn the boats behind me, and just go full on for the lifestyle that I knew was possible. Also legends such as Joel Putland, Mike Dillard, Tim Sales, and Jonathan Budd were and are great to learn from.

Our first big breakthrough came with affiliate marketing, but our eyes were truly opened by the "new age" of network marketing. Internet marketers were making eight-figure incomes using this business model.

Believe in Yourself and in What You Are Doing

I had tried network marketing before with limited success. But since then, the Internet had matured: online speeds were faster, and things like video, Facebook, Skype, webinars, and blogs allowed us to bring our personalities, words, and faces into people's homes and build trust and relationships. People looking for an opportunity could find us instead of us having to find them.

I had always believed in myself, and I knew throughout the tough times of getting this business off the ground that I would achieve my goals. But believing in yourself isn't enough if you don't believe in what you are doing. I believed in this powerful business model, and we built our business quickly and profitably.

Lead by Example

One of the main reasons to believe 100% in what you are doing is that you inspire those you lead to do the same. People will do what you do, not what you say, and with network marketing, my success relies on the success of the people I lead. They won't try anything I'm not willing to try.

When you believe in your product or service, you will be a natural salesperson. You won't be able to stop talking about it. Your enthusiasm will infect everyone around you, from other marketers to potential clients. If you do not believe in what you are doing, no one else will either. If this is the case for you, if you are not passionate every day about what you're doing, then go back to step one. It's time for a new dream, one that excites you and scares you, one that you can believe in.

Take Responsibility and Never Give Up

No matter what happens in your life, you are responsible for your successes *and* your failures. Every time I blamed someone else when something went wrong, I delayed my success. It does not matter whether you are justified in placing blame, doing so will always take your destiny out of your own hands. Figure out what you *do* control and focus on that.

While building our company, there were tears, fights, near bankruptcy, working around the clock at times, doubts, hissy fits, sacrifices, wanting to quit, abuse, let downs, bad days, and good days. But in the end, only one thing mattered—we never quit. That in essence is why we succeeded while others fell by the wayside.

Time and again, these principles have worked for me. I have achieved my goal of being a millionaire at age 30, and at 32, I'm well on my way to meeting another goal, becoming a multimillionaire by age 35. More importantly, I am living the life of my dreams. You can too.

One of my favorite quotes comes from Henry Ford: "If you think you can . . . or you think you can't . . . you're right."

Your thoughts create the life you live. Success is all in your head— until you act on it.

Biography
Aaron Byerlee

Home Business Expert and cofounder of "The Deck Chair Millionaires," AARON BYERLEE's Ultimate Success came after a long journey of entrepreneurial adventures, as most successful people can identify with. After reading *Rich Dad, Poor Dad* by Robert Kiyosaki at age 22, he got into business and the journey began. After buying, building ,and selling three fitness clubs from the ages of 22 to 32 as well as buying seven properties, he turned his attention to the Internet. Although already successful, this business model took his success to a new level. But more importantly, it gave him the leverage and residual income that provided him with the dream lifestyle he was seeking. This was in the form of what he calls "The New Age Of Network Marketing"—the most powerful and leveraged business model for residual income. Today he lives his passion of coaching others to find and live their ultimate lifestyles.

Contact Information

www.AaronByerlee.com
www.Facebook.com/aaronbyerlee
aaron@HomeBusinessExpert4U.com

Chapter 9

Love Is Success

by Wendy Estevez-Amara

I remember it like it was yesterday, hearing the words come out of the psychologist's mouth, "Wendy, you are bipolar." It wasn't, "We think you are bipolar," or "There is a possibility you have a bipolar condition." It was, "Wendy, you are bipolar." The words stuck to me like a huge Post-it note placed on my forehead. It sounded so final. Was this doctor telling me I was mentally ill? Oh no . . . is that really what he was saying? Suddenly my whole life flashed before my eyes. All my dreams of one day getting married, having children, making a difference in the lives of others, working in a profession I was proud of—all slowly melted away, like the witch at the end of the *Wizard of Oz* when she gets water thrown on her. I'm melting, I'm melting, I'm melting. . . .

This diagnosis and my resistance to simply accepting it began my journey of self-discovery. At first the doctors recommended some medications for me, and although I took three different medications over two years, I felt no difference in my energy level or mood swings.

I realized then that I had to look within for the solution. That I had to be really honest with myself about what I was feeling and what was going on in my soul. I took my first steps by entering the world of personal transformation.

It has now been close to 10 years since I first heard that misleading diagnosis and began my journey. Today I am a confident, loving, honest, authentic, and joyful woman. I no longer believe that I was ever "bipolar." I was just out of tune with my soul and unaligned with my spirit. What I needed was a good adjustment and realignment. By taking an honest look at myself, I began the work of finding my spirit again and getting clear on what really mattered to me. This is what I discovered.

At the end of the day, what really mattered to me were the people around me, the love I felt for them and the love I received from them. As long as I was open to being loved and fully loving others, I felt aligned with the universe. I also discovered that I had to learn to love myself. After much soul searching, I realized that love is really all there is and that a successful life is a life full of love. Success to me is defined as being consciously aware of the experience of love and self-love in my life.

You might be thinking, *But it can't all be about love. It can't be that simple.* Love is one central experience we are all looking for. All other feelings, emotions, and experiences really do stem from it. Freedom comes from love, joy comes from love, courage comes from love, forgiveness comes from love, gratitude comes from love, even confidence stems from love. If you take any human emotion that you are searching for or wanting in your life, at its core you can always find love.

Love and the full experience of it enhances every area of your life, even in areas of life that seem far from this emotion, such as finances or work. When you are fully present to who loves you and whom you love, your financial decisions seem to fall into place. Work commitments have a deeper meaning when you are clearly connected to the reason behind why you are doing them, usually connected to the love of your family. If you dig deep enough, behind every motive you have or action you take, you can find love. We are usually not consciously aware of it.

You might be asking, *How did I come to this conclusion?* In searching how to heal myself, I found that I felt the happiest and most complete when I was focused on love. So I went in search of love and found that I already had an abundance of it in my life. Everywhere I looked I could find examples of love showing up in my life. Whether it was a call from a friend I hadn't spoken to in a while, or a warm hug from someone at work, love was all around me. And not just from those we expect love from, such as our families. All I had to do was open my eyes, and suddenly I saw love everywhere. I saw love in the bank teller who helped me at the bank, in my neighbor who smiled and said hello as we passed each other, in my co-worker who asked how I was doing.

I also experienced, for the first time, true unconditional love for myself. This came to me in an interesting way. Once I was focused on finding love in my life, I began to see the love that came through nature. I remember staring at a tree and being in awe of how God had created something so beautiful. I actually felt love coming from this tree. The more time I spent in nature, the more I felt love coming through the flowers, the plants, the trees, everything. When I really opened my arms to this love and accepted it, I began to love myself more and more. I felt that if I was surrounded by so much love from nature, I must be worth being loved. It was an interesting awareness. I began to feel unconditional love for myself. It was like a magical experience. Everything made sense, and for the first time in my life, I felt truly aligned with the universe.

After this experience, I decided I wanted to find a partner to share my life with. I had dated many men before but had never dated with this newfound awareness. I made a commitment to myself that I would be open to this love entering my life. It wasn't an easy process, but through the thick and thin of it, I stayed committed and focused on the one thing I knew I had discovered was central to my life, *love*.

The process was long and once again focused mostly on my own self-growth, but in the end, I found the love of my life. Yes! Love came into my life. I attracted it and have now been married for over four years to one of the most beautiful, loving, giving men on earth. This didn't happen from one day to the next. It took 32 dates over a year and a half to find him. Talk about committed! I stayed open to the process even through some not-so-great dates. What I discovered was that my biggest struggle had nothing to do with the men who where showing up and everything to do with the box I had created for what love should look like. I was able to break through that box and connect to what really mattered in my partner.

Also through this dating process I found that I wasn't alone in wanting to find love. There were and still are many other woman and men out there who want to find the love of their life and for whatever reason are finding it harder than they expected. I learned some valuable lessons along the way and realized that I could share these lessons with others in search of love.

This brought me to life coaching. I have coached many individuals over the last six years. Most recently, over the last two years, I have coached individuals searching for love and have been successful in helping them find it. I currently have two clients who are engaged and getting married next year! It's been a very exciting process for me to share my journey and the tools I picked up along the way. At the end of the day, when all the other definitions of success are stripped to the core, what you find is love.

My journey has been a long and treacherous one, and I am most grateful for every challenge, breakthrough, and insight I have gained. All of this has affected my day-to-day life in that I realize success is a choice every minute of every day. For me it is a choice of being consciously aware of love in my life in the present moment, especially during difficult times. Success has come to me in my life due to a consistent practice of conscious awareness of love. You can find this success too. All it takes is practice.

The steps I have found that work are:

1. *Be consciously and consistently aware of the love that already surrounds you.* Notice the daily miracles of love that are happening in your life right now, like getting kisses from your kids, or having someone give you a parking space at a crowded mall. When you really start looking for how many moments of love surround you, you feel like the richest person on earth.

2. *Be consciously and consistently aware of the love coming to you from nature, God, the universe, spirit, or whatever name you choose for your higher power.* Spend time in nature; spend time communing with your higher power—meditating, praying, yoga, or whatever works for you.

3. *Be consciously and consistently aware of the love you feel for others.* Let your heart swell up with the unconditional love you feel for your children, your family, your friends, and your community. Show this love to them through your actions.

4. *Be consciously and consistently aware of loving yourself.* This can be the most difficult of all. Take the time to acknowledge your daily accomplishments. Treat yourself to something nice every once in a while. Most importantly, remind yourself of how truly special and unique you are. The more you love yourself, the more love will enter your life.

These are the steps that have led me to success in my life. Ten years ago I thought that none of my goals or dreams would come to fruition. I was stuck in the diagnosis box of "bipolar." Today I am clear that I was never really bipolar—just disconnected from what matters most in life. With a simple shift of attention to what truly matters, my life has flourished. I consider myself successful, not simply because I have love in life, but more important, because I choose in every moment to consciously and consistently be aware of the gift of that love. If you focus on love, and the abundance of love in your life, and truly loving yourself, everything else will fall into place.

I am grateful for those around me who have taught me the meaning of love. My parents, who continue to amaze me through their unconditional love; my cousin Suki, who continues to challenge me; and my husband, Joey, who has been my biggest teacher. I have learned that love is the highest vibration, and that it is the biggest gift we can give others and ourselves.

Biography

Wendy Estevez-Amara

WENDY ESTEVEZ-AMARA is currently a life coach, specializing in coaching woman and men searching for love. She lives with her husband, Joseph Amara, in Santa Clarita, California. Wendy has a B.A. in sociology from UCLA and a life coaching certificate from the Breakthrough Coaching Academy through Mastery in Transformational Training (MITT). She has coached over 500 people in achieving personal goals, finding their life purpose, and living from a place of what is truly important.

Contact Information

www.coachwendyamara.com
coachingurlife@gmail.com
Cell: 818-395-2645

Chapter 10

Becoming the Man in the Arena

by Mikel Erdman

I grew up on a farm in southwestern Oregon, in a very small town named Bandon. It's famous now because a rich guy from Chicago came and built some of the top-rated golf courses in the world there. When I was growing up, it was nothing like that. It was a sleepy coastal town surviving on the final feast of the logging and fishing industries and very little else.

My dad was in the meat business just like his father before him, and his father before him. In the summers we fished our commercial salmon troller for Chinook and Coho salmon and occasionally took off after albacore tuna if they came close enough to shore. Working these businesses successfully meant long hours and sore muscles and a lot of ingenuity and resourcefulness to stay afloat.

I was surrounded by hard work growing up—the kind of hard and dirty work they would feature on the television show *Dirty Jobs*. In fact, these were the types of jobs that you had to have a whole different set of clothes for work than you'd ever wear for anything else. It was next to impossible to get the smells out once you'd worn them around the feedlot or in the back end of the boat, with diesel fumes and fish innards and cow manure as the benefits of the position.

From as early as I can remember I was doing chores and participating in the family businesses. Just growing up in that small business, do-it-yourself atmosphere had a lot to do with me achieving a high level of success in my life. I learned many lessons about dealing with adversity and rising to the challenge.

I saw the magic of new ideas formulated in the mind and then brought to reality by the power of vision, dedication, and persistence. And I learned one of the most important lessons about success right there in the middle of those hard, dirty jobs—that not all good ideas work out, and true success comes to those who are willing to face their failures and step out once again to achieve their dreams.

In fact, if you look at some of the most successful people in the world, their careers never shoot to the top without any challenges or setbacks along the way. Some of the most respected and revered leaders in our land seemed to have just a long string of failures accentuated by moments of greatness and, more than anything, characterized by the unwillingness to ever give up or give in.

Take this person for example:

He was born into poverty and early in his life, his family was broke and forced out of their home. He had to work as a child to support them. His mother passed away when he was only 9 years old. By 22 he had started and failed in his own business. Shortly thereafter he ran for public office and lost, then started a second business, which failed within two years . . . on borrowed money. A few years later his fiancée died unexpectedly, and he suffered a complete nervous breakdown.

Throughout his life he lost eight separate elections, but in 1860 he was finally elected president of the United States of America. Who was he? Mr. Abraham Lincoln

Abe Lincoln is one of the most revered leaders in all of American history. When you look at the record of his life, however, you'd be hard pressed to believe in his greatness, up until the point that he successfully led his country through one of the most critical periods of its existence. What if he had given up? What if he had quit after the first business failure?

It's clear that Mr. Lincoln's failures did not define the altitude of his achievement. And this point is true for you too! It's one of the hardest lessons to learn and is critical to your success in life. You have the power to change. You have the power to make course corrections throughout your life and learn from the challenges that you encounter along your journey. You, and only you, can give yourself permission to use that wisdom to move forward and make your mark on the world.

Growing up in an entrepreneurial environment and seeing this cycle of success and failure consistently play out led me to understand that a singular defeat doesn't cause you to lose the game of life. Your success is based on your own willingness to get up off the ground, dust yourself off, and get back into the game. You must understand that it's just part of the process and isn't unique to you.

In my own life, I've had to overcome a few large failures myself. I once started a real estate advertising technology firm that took off like a rocket ship. We had developed a novel technology product that made a lot of sense in the marketplace and added a lot of value to the businesses of real estate agents, mortgage lenders, and other real estate professionals who used our systems. We grew the company from zero, with no outside investment, to over $1 million in sales, and from 2 to

35 employees within 18 months. I thought we'd hit the big one—and I was only 33 years old at the time.

There were a lot of expenses, but the cash flow was great, and it looked like we had it made. This was the first time in my life that I really knew what it meant to have no money troubles at all. We were completely debt-free except our home, and we had plenty of reserves stashed away. We literally had more money than we knew what to do with.

I wish I could tell you that the fairy tale lasted, the business continued to grow, and we rode off into the sunset with our bags of riches. It didn't, and we didn't. In the second winter, the business changed—fast. The technology that our business was based on completely revolutionized within two years, making much what we delivered irrelevant. And the employees and overhead didn't slow down at the same rate as the revenue coming in.

They say that the larger a ship is the longer it takes to slow it down or change course. That is absolutely true in business. We had reinvested all the sales revenue we had made in the run-up of the company, and the overhead started to eat us alive. We ended up closing the company at the three-year mark with hundreds of thousands of dollars in personal investment lost.

Let me tell you something: that hurt. I mean it physically hurt. I was crushed. I had poured three years of my life working up to 16 hours a day to make this dream come true. I had a serious case of self-doubt that I could ever make anything successful again. I mean, if you had something so powerful that took off so fast and made so much money while doing an incredible amount of good in the world and you lost it all, wouldn't you question your ability to make it happen again?

It took a couple of months to start feeling better after that failure, but the resilience that I had learned back on the farm showed up, and I set my sights on the next chapter of my life. I got busy and came up with a new plan. I set out to reinvent myself. I had to pull myself and my family out of this financial wasteland. Over the next three years, I went on to have the highest personal income years in my entire career.

What would have happened if I'd given up? Sure, I had a lot of reasons to just lie on the couch and throw a big pity party. A lot of people would have understood why I wasn't achieving anything after seeing that huge swing-and-a-miss. In fact, a few did tell me that maybe I should just lie low, you know, get a safe and secure job and give up on those big dreams. But I knew, down deep in my heart, that the failure of that one business couldn't define who I was in the world and the value that I could continue to bring people in so many ways.

It's the same way for you too! No matter what trials and tribulations you've faced on your journey thus far, you can decide right here and now that you're going on to bigger and better things. You can set your sights on the pinnacle of your own personal achievement, and with commitment, hard work, and persistence, you can make those dreams into reality.

Most importantly, each and every one of you has everything it takes to achieve your goals. You have been given the most powerful computer, a flawless operating system, and the most incredible architecture ever known on the face of the Earth since the day you were created. It's up to you to harness that power and make a decision to accomplish your dreams.

Recently, as we were celebrating the New Year and looking forward to the great events and successes to come in the year ahead, I had a startling and somewhat chilling revelation. This was not just a new year; this was a new decade. A new *decade*! At the end of this decade, I would be nearing 50 years old, my children would be most of the way through their school years and off to college, and I would have come upon the time in my life when I had always dreamed of being retired early and traveling the world. I gulped hard and felt my hands get a little clammy.

What would I accomplish in this new era of my life? I had been in this position many times, but the nervousness never quite goes away, that familiar dark, turning feeling in the pit of my stomach that asks, "Mikel, are you up to the challenge?"

I decided right then that this decade would be the most productive era of my life and that I would dedicate myself to planning and executing better than ever before. You see, that has been one of the most critical secrets to my success, and it's the same with every other successful person I've ever met, listened to, or read about. The willingness to face head-on the uneasiness and uncertainty of challenging circumstances is the hallmark of a true leader.

Napoleon Hill, one of the greatest thought leaders who ever lived, said it best: "Whatever the mind can conceive and believe, the mind can achieve."

James Nesmith had a dream of improving his golf game, and he developed a unique method of achieving his goal. Until he devised this method, he was just your average weekend golfer, shooting in the mid to low 90s. Then, for seven years, he completely quit the game. He never touched a club. He never set foot on a fairway.

Ironically, it was during this seven-year break that he came up with his amazingly effective technique for improving his game—a technique we can all learn from. In fact, the first time he set foot on a golf course after his hiatus, he shot an astonishing 74. He cut 20 strokes off his average without having swung a golf club in seven years. Unbelievable! Not only that, but his physical condition had actually deteriorated during those seven years.

What was his secret? Visualization. You see, Major Nesmith had spent those seven years as a prisoner of war in North Vietnam. During those seven years, he was imprisoned in a cage that was approximately four and one-half feet high and five feet long.

During almost the entire time he was imprisoned, he saw no one, talked to no one, and experienced no physical activity. During the first few months, he did virtually nothing but hope and pray for his release. Then he realized he had to find some way to occupy his mind or he would lose his sanity and probably his life. That's when he learned the power of building his future in his mind's eye.

In his mind, he selected his favorite golf course and started playing golf. Every day, he played a full 18 holes at the imaginary country club of his dreams. He experienced everything to the last detail. He saw himself dressed in his golfing clothes. He smelled the fragrance of the trees and the freshly trimmed grass. He experienced different weather conditions—windy spring days, overcast winter days, and sunny summer mornings.

In his imagination, every detail of the tee, the individual blades of grass, the trees, the singing birds, the scampering squirrels, and the lay of the course became totally real.

He felt the grip of the club in his hands. He instructed himself as he practiced smoothing out his down-swing and the follow-through on his shot. Then he watched the ball arc down the exact center of the fairway, bounce a couple of times, and roll to the exact spot he had selected, all in his mind.

In the real world, he was in no hurry. He had no place to go. So in his mind he took every step on his way to the ball, just as if he were physically on the course. It took him just as long in imaginary time to play 18 holes as it would have taken in reality. Not a detail was omitted. Not once did he ever miss a shot, never a hook or slice, nor miss a putt.

Eighteen holes of golf every day, seven days a week, for seven years. Twenty strokes off his score for a lifetime best score of 74.

Here are the questions for all of us as we start our new decade:

- What are you visualizing?
- What do you have your mind focused on, and where is that focus taking you?

Without a clear vision of where you are going, you're likely to get lost along the way. You may end up looking back at the beginning of 2020 wondering which road you took and how you arrived where you are.

It's your choice. It all comes down to a few simple planning steps and daily committed action in the direction of your dreams.

1. Fix in your mind the exact goal or desire in your life.
2. Determine exactly what you intend to give in return for the achievement of your goal.
3. Establish a definite date for the achievement of the goal.
4. Create a definite plan for carrying out your desire and begin at once, whether you are ready or not, to put this plan into action.
5. Write a clear and concise statement including the exact goal, what you intend to give in return, the time limit for its achievement, and the plan through which you intend to succeed.
6. Read your written statement aloud a minimum of twice daily, once immediately after arising in the morning, and once again immediately before retiring at night.

In closing, I'd like to leave you with two comments. The first is that your failures don't define you and can't defeat you unless you let them. Failure is simply a reflection point on your way to your ultimate destination. Failures are an opportunity to learn what to do better next time and to develop the wisdom that you'll need to positively affect the lives of many.

Second, I want you to know that taking a step into the unknown on faith is purely courageous. If you have a desire to become more in the world, if you have a song in your heart that has not been released to the wind, if you have a blessing inside you waiting to burst out, showing your greatness to the world, then get moving. Don't waste a single moment worrying about what might happen if you fail. Do everything in your power to avoid failure, but accept setbacks as part of the process of achieving your dreams.

One of our cherished American leaders, Teddy Roosevelt, reminds us that the person of action and determination is to be admired:

"It is not the critic who counts; not the man who points out how the strong man stumbles, or where the doer of deeds could have done them better. The credit belongs to the man who is actually in the arena, whose face is marred by dust and sweat and blood; who strives valiantly; who errs, who comes short again and again, because there is no effort without error and shortcoming; but who does actually strive to do the deeds; who knows great enthusiasms, the great devotions; who spends himself in a worthy cause; who at the best knows in the end the triumph of high achievement, and who at the worst, if he fails, at least fails while daring greatly, so that his place shall never be with those cold and timid souls who neither know victory nor defeat."

Biography

Mikel Erdman

MIKEL ERDMAN has been engaging and inspiring sales and marketing professionals for more than 15 years. A product of the success principles he teaches, Mikel started his entrepreneurial career immediately after graduating from college. He became a self-made millionaire by the age of 30 and has successfully started and grown multiple companies in the mortgage, technology, and advertising arenas.

Contact Information

www.mikelerdman.com

360-450-3551

Chapter 11

Human Being vs. Human Doing

by Alex Urbina

*A*s a transformational family life coach, I facilitate trainings and workshops for teens, parents, and families all across the world. I help teens and parents reconnect with their heart, discover their inner truth, and remember who they are through experiential learning. The trainings are an abrupt intervention in self-pity and victimization, guiding the youth to discover their personal power by taking responsibility for where they are in their lives. I create a safe space for them to complete their past, learn how to live in the moment, and stand as the source for creating their unforeseen future.

Seventeen years ago, I embarked on a life-altering journey of self-awareness and leadership. An immediate result of this passage was the creation of my own personal vision statement; I didn't know it at the time, but it would faithfully lead me through my life. I wanted a vision that was way bigger than me; I wanted it to be the legacy I would leave behind for my children, my grandchildren, and the world to remember me by.

I, Alex Urbina, am committed to living my life with passion and purpose, to making a difference in the world by helping others to discover their greatness. I am committed to finding my own light and giving away the gift that I am to the world. I stand as the source of love and the pursuit of inner truth for all of my brothers and sisters who are ready to hear it.

To me, defining success is entirely internal; it is within one's ability to just *be* independent from achieving, accomplishing, or "having" anything. Most people think that when they achieve, accomplish, or have a thing, it will bring them the experience they associate with it. But those types of experiences—like freedom, passion, love, security, confidence, power, and happiness—are all accessible within us; they are not acquired from something outside us.

All of those experiences are ways of *being,* and when you figure out how to master those ways of being from within, you will attract the opportunities to achieve, accomplish, or have.

Your soul does not care what you do, and it certainly does not care what you accomplish or achieve. It only cares about who you are being while you do whatever it is that you do in life. When you access certain ways of being, an extraordinary way of living will spring forth that will be rich, fulfilling, and magnificently abundant.

Do you not think that someone who figures out how to truly be powerful, passionate, loving, and confident will not be externally successful? These types of people eventually draw external success to them.

This concept might be different than what most people are used to and difficult for some people to accept. Most people's idea of success has to do with what happens outside them. It's the kind of success that comprises earning a lot of money, attaining status, and acquiring material things.

In my early years in the field of personal transformation, among the many people I coached, I often had some overachievers, super accomplished and financially successful people, on my teams.

They were all seeking to *be* genuinely happy, to *be* passionate about what they did, to *be* loved in their relationships, to *be* fulfilled with what they had, to *be* secure in who they were, and to find their purpose in life.

The rest of the people I coached all wanted to achieve some goals, accomplish something great, and reach financial success—all so that they could *be* genuinely happy, *be* passionate about what they did, *be* loved in their relationships, *be* fulfilled with what they had, *be* secure in who they were, and to find their purpose in life.

At the end of the day, what people are really after is to live and feel extraordinary. People want to deeply experience the awe of who they are. And this fulfilling experience does not come from what you do or what you have—it comes from who you choose to be in each moment.

The single most important key to achieving success for me was undoubtedly The Wake-Up Call. First I needed to be willing to be wrong about all my opinions and what I thought I knew. Second, I needed to be willing to take an honest look at myself. And third, I needed to be willing to open my heart and trust all that came from it.

From there I was able to see and experience who I really am. I was inspired and moved deeply by it—I would never *be* the same because of this experience. It sprouted a new life for me, a new beginning. I went on to learn how to be a true leader, to take full responsibility for my life, to discover my own power and purpose, and to realize the gift I am to the world.

From this realization came some of the steps I use for achieving success:

- I am constantly and regularly checking in with myself—a self-awareness, an ongoing assessment of what I am feeling and what it is that I want to experience next.

- I have developed a way to listen to my soul for my truth, and when I seek answers, I often listen to the messages it sends me. I use my brain only for information and data.

- I focus more on who I am being in each moment than on what I need to do, and this allows me to experience true freedom; I live life with minimal stress and little to no pressure. This powerful energy of who I am being in each moment produces its own "to do" list, so before I can think of what I need to do, it is already obvious.

- Because I have discovered my passion, I live a purpose-driven life, and that ultimately rewards me with a deep sense of gratitude and many other extraordinary blessings and opportunities that keep showing up.

- I have completed my past, which gives me the freedom to live in the moment and create new experiences from pure intention and the power of now.

- I am really clear about certain leadership distinctions and some universal laws that allow me to have a unique perspective on life. I see a world of unlimited possibilities, and I see options that most people cannot—not because I am any more special than they are, but only because I have practiced more than they have.

- I am constantly and rigorously remembering who I am through my contribution to the world and being of service to others.

- I focus more on building relationships with people and less on what's in it for me.

• I have spent and still spend money, time, and practice on my personal and spiritual growth as if my life depends on it.

In my 17 years on a transformational journey, I have come to many conclusions. One is that all life's challenges, mishaps, and mistakes are blessings. Most people try to avoid making mistakes, or even taking the risks associated with the growth process that awaits them on the other side. I have taught myself how to enjoy the process of learning from my mistakes. I have chosen to view them as stepping stones for success.

As a life coach, we call them breakdowns, and without a breakdown, breakthroughs are not possible.

The more I am willing to see mistakes as opportunities for growth, the more I embrace them as they appear. I did this repeatedly for years until one day I looked at myself and noticed a few things.

I noticed that I no longer gave up my power in those moments, that I no longer resisted what showed up, that my perspective had changed dramatically. In every challenging moment or roadblock that fell before me, I was able to see many possible ways around it. I was able to see things that I could not see before, and more importantly, I started to notice that all those challenging moments, roadblocks, and failures, as some of you call them, had nothing to do with who I am.

I am a powerful, passionate, and loving leader! Leadership to me is everything. Leadership to me is living your life to serve others. It is a responsibility to God to take the gift that you are and *be* a contribution to the world, in whatever it is that you are passionate about.

The qualities that make a great leader are authenticity, compassion, and confidence. Authenticity is being true to one's own spirit, personality, or character, and to me that speaks louder than words. Compassion is being connected to your heart; it blossoms from a deeply loving place within yourself, and it usually shows up through empathy and sympathy for the suffering of others. This quality to me is the driving force that causes action. Confidence is knowing the gift that you are; it's a higher belief in your own power, your ability and assurance in what it is that you have to offer. What you do as a leader is usually born out of who you are being.

My all-time favorite quote on success:

*It is true that when you achieve certain states of being
over a long period of time, success in what you are doing in the world
is difficult to avoid. Yet you are not to worry about 'Making a Living.'
True masters are those who have chosen to make a life,
rather than a living.*
—Neale Donald Walsch

This quote for me says it all; it explains how powerful we are as human *beings* and what we should focus on. It is all about faith.

I have many mentors in my life, and all for different reasons: God, who is constantly reminding me that I am love; my parents, Alex and Gloria, because they love me unconditionally; my wife, Yvette, and my children, Mark, Jazmine, and Sasha, because they believe in me no matter what; Kathy and Sue because before I could see what a gift I was to the world, they saw it first and made damn sure that I saw it too; and Dr. Ray for being my spiritual brother and my inspirational role model—he leads with his heart and inspires me to leave my own legacy and imprint on the world.

Biography

Alex R. Urbina

Have you ever dreamed of living your life with a purpose, and being rewarded for it in ways that you could not imagine? ALEX URBINA is fulfilling that dream. In 1994 at the age of twenty-three, he had a profound and unique experience that changed his life forever. Since then, he has been making a difference in communities and families all over the world. Today he is a transformational life coach, recognized as one of the leading experts in Transformational Trainings for teens and parents abroad.

He encourages families all over the world to step into his trainings, where small but extraordinary miracles take place, where people in team-like settings feel safe enough to open their hearts, discover their inner truth, and remember who they are. Urbina's vision is forever growing, and his ultimate intention is to restore the family values that seem to be fading away in our rapidly changing world. He is always working on new ways to reach the masses, and he is on a mission to be all-loving and do whatever it takes to have this movement hit critical mass.

Contact Information

www.alexurbina.com
alex@alexurbina.com
805-551-9742

Chapter 12

Creating Authentic Partnership
SUCCESS WITH AND
THROUGH HONORING PEOPLE

by Dawnelle J. Hyland

What life continues to reveal to me is that sustainable success comes when I value and respect people, and, in return, they experience themselves as respected and valued in my presence. I believe that, at heart, every human being wants to be understood—that is, validated for the unique ways about them, the talents, attributes, perspectives, and experiences that have shaped who they are, and the vision and concerns that shape who they are becoming. When people feel acknowledged in this way, even if we don't quite see eye to eye on particular *matters* at hand, we are able to see *each other*. From here, people are far more willing to stay the course and put their heart into whatever we are partnering in together. This holds true whether people have come together to create a business, a marriage, a friendship, a project, or any endeavor that calls for full commitment from all involved.

This lesson came together for me when, several years ago, I had the honor of leading a middle school through a full-scale transformation. This project had special meaning for me, as it was the school in which I had previously taught.

At the time, the school was, at best, a dreary place to be. It had fallen into a decade-long pattern of students performing well below grade level according to state standards. Students and teachers were often at odds, feeling disrespected by one another. This lack of connection was reflected in several students being suspended from school, large turnover rates among teachers, graffiti on school walls, students and teachers yelling at one another, and the like. There was an overall feel of mediocrity and resignation in the air, and a distinct context of "if it's to be, it's up to someone else."

Transforming this school's culture was a large commitment and required full heart and buy-in from a critical mass of our faculty. To create something there that none of us had experienced before required that we step into the unknown with one another—an uncomfortable prospect.

As we began the journey, my initial goals were to assist the faculty in unifying around a vision and mission that inspired them, and to bring a spirit of respect and honor to the way they interacted with one another and with students. With that foundation in place, we could build consistency around infrastructure and best practices that would lead to the results we wanted. I held many retreats, workshops, and meetings wherein teachers had the opportunity to engage fully in the process.

For the first eight months of this four-year process, I met with what seemed at the time like resistance from a long-standing member of the faculty, "Joe" (not his real name). He either didn't attend meetings at all, or in the few meetings he did attend, he was vocal about why he didn't think whatever was being suggested or requested at the time would work. When asked for his ideas about solutions, he would make statements like "Well, it won't matter. This will all fall apart like every other new initiative does." He also held "water cooler" conversations with other faculty members about why he didn't support the work we were doing.

Joe had been at the school for nearly 27 years, since its opening. He was well respected among faculty. As his influence spread, our progress stalled. Faculty members initially excited about the transformation began to have doubts. Conversations turned from "what can we really create together here" to "here are all the reasons why it won't work, and I'm not sure I want to participate." Energy at meetings flattened, and I felt we had taken a giant step backwards.

In the face of this, I began to see and relate to Joe as an outsider—separate from what we were doing. He was a thorn in my side, the enemy, a saboteur. Furthermore, I questioned his intentions. I found myself thinking he had an agenda to have his way so that, ultimately, he wouldn't have to try new approaches that might be uncomfortable and require personal risk. Although there may have been some truth to this, rather than having compassion for him, I had disdain. I decided that he was more concerned about looking good than about the future of our students. I fell victim to him. He was the reason the project wasn't working. From there, I could make no difference.

I avoided him and tried to work around him as well as the others who had fallen into the same ways of thinking. This wasn't effective..

As I stepped back from the situation, it dawned on me that, with Joe, I wasn't being true to the spirit of respect and honor that I had committed to creating in the school. In the literal sense, "respect" means "re-see." I began to "re-see" Joe by questioning my initial interpretations about him: What if he did really care? What does he bring to the table that I haven't been willing to honor?

As I asked myself these questions, the tension I was feeling fell away. I felt a lightness and a renewed energy. I started to put myself in his shoes. He was an elective teacher, and up until then, because students were not tested in extracurricular subject areas, elective teachers were often an afterthought when it came to making big decisions that affected the school. I could see how he might feel marginalized, as though on some level, who he was or what he brought to the table didn't matter.

Once an enemy, Joe became an ally in my eyes. Once a man with his own agenda, he now seemed more like a man who cared deeply. After all, he had stuck it out for 27 years in a school many had left within a short time.

I invited him into my office to have a conversation. I acknowledged his care in speaking up and owned up to recognizing that he must have been trying to communicate something to me that I hadn't heard. I also acknowledged that as an elective teacher, he must have felt marginalized. As I shared with him, his tough façade melted with a few tears. Finally, someone got him. Someone was hearing him.

As we talked and shared perspectives, it was evident that we didn't see eye to eye on all counts. I learned to appreciate our diversity as an asset to the work we were doing. His perspectives were unique, and by validating them, we had more information from which to make key decisions.

After our conversation, he joined our Leadership Team and became instrumental in getting the rest of the faculty on board with significant transformations being made in the school, most notably those teachers who had heretofore felt left out and taken an apathetic path of least resistance.

All 100 of us, working together in a spirit of authentic partnership, achieved extraordinary results. We moved from under 40% to over 95% of students performing at or above grade level. School approval ratings shot up on district and statewide assessments. Most importantly, the culture became one in which students and teachers were proud to work and learn.

Creating authentic partnership, especially with those who appear to be dissenters, is often easier said than done. It looks like it is about them, but my experience has shown me that creating partnership is actually an inside job.

Here are three intertwined and fundamental practices that can lead to successful partnerships through honoring:

1. **Make a distinction between who a person *is* and how a person *acts*.**

    It is human nature to create characterizations of people based on what we see them do and why we think they are doing it. In other words, we ascribe motives to their behaviors and often confuse their identity with their behaviors and our assumptions about their motives. When partnership is out, our characterizations are keeping it out.

    So, this practice involves recognizing that your leverage in any situation is the meaning, or set of interpretations, that you bring to it.

    In my example, what Joe *factually did* was (1) speak up in and outside of meetings about why he didn't think what we were doing would work, and (2) not participate in some things we asked people to do.

    What I *interpreted* was that he wanted his way so he wouldn't have to make changes. I told myself a story that his surface opposition was really a cover-up for his desire to stay comfortable and not have to face the unknown.

    Inside this story, Joe was for me a saboteur, the enemy. I related to that interpretation by avoiding him and attempting to work around him. Hence, our progress stalled.

When I questioned my initial interpretations, a new Joe emerged—Joe the ally. In turn, I related to him as a partner by acknowledging I hadn't been hearing him and asking him to share his perspective. Hence, we worked together to accomplish extraordinary results.

2. Stand in partnership.

"Standing in" anything involves having faith that it is there, already available to you—an "of course," even in the face of no recognizable evidence at a particular moment.

It requires that you do what may seem counterintuitive: recognize that the interpretations you have about a person or situation are driving what is and is not available to you. This is what I meant above when I said partnership is an inside job.

A key principle here is that there is no "world out there." There is no fixed reality. Often, as human beings, we believe that the way we *see* people or events is the way that they *are*— in other words, people and events are fixed, unalterable. This positions us to be a victim to others, as I was to Joe. It also positions us to experience ourselves as bound and limited. As long as I saw him as a saboteur, I could make no difference

To stand in something, consciously, is to recognize that the world is not *fixed* but *occurring*. You may have had a time in your life when you saw someone one way, and another person saw that same person a different way, and each of your relationships, with the same person, were very different. This is because people and events literally present themselves in our lives as consistent with our interpretations.

So, standing in partnership, consciously, involves choosing interpretations that line up with being a partner and having partners around you. When I chose to question my initial views about Joe and return to my original intention of creating an honoring and respectful culture, I saw him through new eyes and was with him in a distinct way. I became a partner in the act of relating to him as a partner.

The more you practice doing this consciously, the more it will become natural, like breathing. There will come a time when simply *being* a partner, and thus, creating partners all around you, will become as second nature as driving your car.

Let me pause for a moment and be clear that I am not suggesting you be naïve. Some of you reading may be wondering: "But what if Joe *really had* an agenda and wasn't coming from partnership himself, inside his own world? Isn't that possible?"

Yes, it is possible, but it is also irrelevant. Sincerely relating to Joe as gift, hearing a care and desire to contribute underneath his complaints, opened doors that otherwise would not have been opened. It brought into the foreground the aspect of him that cared deeply, and any hidden agenda he may have had fell away. It also brought me forward as a compassionate, committed ally. This is the power of a stand! When I stand in something that contributes to others, I access the best in myself and bring out the best in others.

3. **Ask yourself questions to keep you on track with your stand. In other words, do a "consciousness check-in."**

   Here are some questions you may ask yourself to bring about powerful partnerships in every domain in your life:
   - Are people honored when I communicate with them?
   - Do people leave an interaction with me with a greater appreciation that *who they are* is a gift, freed up to share

themselves fully, access their talents, and become aware of their inner resources, which perhaps have been dormant?

• Are people uplifted in my space?

Creating successful partnerships is truly in the eyes and beingness of the beholder. What are you beholding today?

Biography

Dawnelle J. Hyland

Founder of Align Leadership, LLC, DAWNELLE J. HYLAND has spent 15 years training and coaching visionary adults and youth to take a quantum leap in realizing their personal and organizational visions as well as to live in a way that honors others and contributes to the quality of life on our planet. Her deep respect for people and their transformation has taken her across the United States and to Ghana, W. Africa, where she has developed leaders in corporations, communities, school districts, government agencies, and nonprofit companies. In 1999, she founded Legacy Leadership for Teens, an experiential program that has had a sustainable impact on the lives of thousands of teens and their families. She is a founding member of the International Coaching, Consulting, and Training Group, a recipient of the prestigious Terry Sanford Award for Innovation and Creativity, and in 2002, she was recognized as a White House Fellows National Finalist. Dawnelle is a transformational trainer, professional development designer, educator, executive coach, author, and speaker who is moved daily by the gifts in people.

Contact Information

www.dawnellehyland.com
www.icctg.com
alignglobal@gmail.com
919-491-4487

Chapter 13

Inspiration
When You Least Expect It

by Brian Mahany

here is a picture on my refrigerator, a picture of a little boy. He is a boy that I have never met, a boy with a bright smile even though he is suffering from an extremely rare and deadly cancer. Why is this picture on my refrigerator? By the end of this story, you will know the answer.

Although I have a large and beautiful home office, I frequently set up my laptop in the kitchen and work there. For many people, the kitchen is the "center" of their home. Across from the kitchen table stands the refrigerator. Like most other homes, our refrigerator does more than just keep food cold; it also serves as a message center and a place to display pictures, artwork, and magnets from trips taken long ago.

There are four pictures on my refrigerator: a Christmas family photo sent by a friend, one of my long ago deceased family pet mastiff, Bear, a picture of my late father taken during World War II, and one of the little boy whose name I do not know.

Our world is filled with many people who struggle through life. They are everywhere. People living paycheck to paycheck. People struggling in dead-end jobs or failing relationships. You don't have to look far to find these people. Some only have to look in the mirror.

The sad reality is that a few will never find happiness or take advantage of a second chance in life. They will never see or seize the opportunities around them, opportunities to do something positive with their lives. From my days as a police officer and later a prosecutor, I have seen many failed lives—people who made the same mistakes repeatedly, who abandoned God or their higher power, who simply gave up hope, or who turned to drugs, crime, or alcohol as their sole salvation.

Thankfully, there are many people around us who make us smile, who motivate us to do better, who offer hope in uncertain times.

Fortunately for me, I have had many successes in life. Career successes, financial freedom, travel, and great family and friends. With all those successes I should have no complaints. But few of us lead fairy tale lives. Misfortune happens to everyone at some point. Disease strikes, businesses fail, relationships falter.

Last year, my streak of good luck hit a rough patch. The firm I worked for fell on financial hard times and suddenly had to let some folks go. As the last hired, I was also the first fired. Ever the optimist, I looked at my sudden loss of work as an opportunity, a chance to start my own law firm.

Eagerly, I began ordering stationery, developing a website, and scouting for new clients. What I did not anticipate were the thousands of other great lawyers also losing their jobs and the large number of recent law school grads who could not find any work in the field.

One very bright young lawyer I know found himself working as a part-time assistant zookeeper in charge of cleaning up after elephants and other large animals. Although he was happy to have a job, this certainly was not the career he had envisioned when enrolling in law school three years earlier.

Just as these lawyers were struggling, so was my new business. My partners and I happened to hang out our shingle during the worst economy in decades.

My earlier enthusiasm soon turned to fear. Without any money for advertising, how could we let clients know of our business and bring them to our door? How would we pay office rent? Our lack of income was beginning to weigh me down.

The legal profession was also changing. New lawyers facing tens of thousands of dollars of unpaid student loans were suddenly advertising rates so ridiculously low that we wondered if clients would even consider paying for our experience.

Each day the fear became worse. How much longer could I keep up with the mortgage? If suddenly finding myself unemployed at age 50 and struggling to start a new practice in the worst economy of my generation was not enough stress in my life, my beloved mother passed away.

With each passing day, the fear became worse, and eventually it turned into depression.

In November 2010, one of my best friends called to ask a favor. Would I accompany him to a fundraiser? I certainly was not thrilled with the idea, particularly with little money to contribute.

I attended more out of a sense of duty and did not know anything about the event other than that it was organized by one of our mutual friends. Once there, I learned that the event was not simply a fundraiser. It was an event to celebrate the life of a young child suffering from a rare and virulent type of cancer. It was a way for the parents to give back to the community and say thanks. It was also an event to raise money for a charity that helps other families of children facing serious illness.

Not until I arrived did I learn how selfless the family was that threw this party. More importantly, not until I arrived did I realize that the little boy was the son of a mutual friend.

On my way to the event, I called my friend and pledged to stay for a few minutes of pleasantries then politely bow out. It was a Friday night after all, and I had plans to share a few cocktails with other friends and watch a game at a sports bar.

Throughout the cocktail hour, the little boy was running around the party. He ran from table to table, surrounded by adults in jackets and dresses, this little boy. He was beaming, taking pictures, and laughing. Surely this could not be the boy suffering from cancer. He was probably the kid of some parents who couldn't find a babysitter that night.

As the dinner began, the lights were dimmed, and a media presentation began about the boy and his family. His doctors told of the months of hospitalization, the pain, and the need for future care; his mother and father (both police officers) told of their efforts to keep the family solvent; and the family thanked the hundreds of caregivers, friends, and neighbors that had rallied behind this little boy. Fellow police officers and neighbors had built a jungle gym in the backyard so the boy could play (he missed months of school and playgrounds). Local businesses helped grant the boy's wish to attend a Milwaukee Bucks basketball game (from the pictures, it looks like the team came through with front row seats).

This little boy who had spent much of his life in the hospital and who faced a very uncertain future was the same little boy who was running around the hotel ballroom smiling and laughing.

Suddenly my plans to "politely bow out" so I could have a beer with friends seemed so unimportant. There would be many opportunities to go out on other nights. I had a great time that night and took home a photo of that little boy and placed it on my refrigerator.

The next morning while eating cereal, I began looking at the other pictures on my refrigerator, in particular, the one of my father, Lieutenant Howard Mahany of the U.S. Army Air Corps, proudly kneeling on the wing of his P-51 Mustang fighter plane. The plane displayed seven flags representing seven enemy aircraft destroyed.

That morning, while looking at the photos on my refrigerator, I learned two important lessons and returned to work on Monday with a renewed sense of energy and a much different perspective on life and work. Happily I can say that since that morning, my fear is in check, my practice is doing very well, and I again remember all those blessings that make me thankful for each day.

What are those two lessons learned that morning?

First, that life is precious. We need to embrace each day and the opportunities each day brings. Life will always throw curve balls now and then. Unfortunately, in these new economic times, people lose their jobs and homes every day. And despite many recent medical miracles, some die. We all will die. The impossible odds faced by that young man suddenly put things in their proper perspective.

If we focus too much on our problems, we lose sight of the opportunities. That boy and his family could have chosen to focus on the pain, the bills, the lost childhood. Instead, they threw a party to thank everyone who had helped them and to provide opportunities for other kids facing life-threatening illness. Don't ever try to tell that child he doesn't have the same opportunities of other kids. In some ways, he has more.

Without energy, inspiration, and motivation, life becomes more difficult. It's not enough to simply love your work. Success is inspired, and sometimes that inspiration can be found in the strangest of places.

Obviously inspiration is more than just a picture on the refrigerator. It's the realization that opportunity is everywhere if you look. I went to work on Monday that week and suddenly found all sorts of opportunities. I find my inspiration from great writers like Matt Morris and Timothy Ferriss. I find inspiration in church. And most of all, I find it through the stories of others, like the little boy on my refrigerator.

I said there were two lessons that next morning, and they are equally important. The other photo on the fridge that provided me with renewed inspiration was that of my father, the World War II fighter pilot and ace. In aerial combat, you survive by killing the enemy before he kills you. It's brutal but that simple.

Fortunately, life for most of us doesn't involve killing, but it does involve action. Anyone can spend their life planning, plotting, and studying. The successful ones among us, however, are those who are also *doing.*

Just like in combat, at some point the planning has to stop and be replaced by action. Reading marketing books, hiring advertising consultants, and developing detailed action plans have their place in any new business. No one should march into battle without a plan.

For many of us, however, we get so wrapped up in the planning that life passes us by before we take the opportunity to act.

As I said before, there are opportunities all around us. To enjoy them, however, we have to take chances and act. Our men and women in Iraq and Afghanistan take huge risks every day. Some pay the ultimate price in the defense of freedom, giving their lives. The risks we take are usually not as deadly, but to have any chance of success, we have to face our fears and take those risks.

What did I learn that day and the next morning? That life offers us inspiration in the most unusual places, and that to succeed, we must not only be inspired but act decisively when opportunity knocks.

By the time this book is published, there will likely be new additions and changes to the outside of our refrigerator—but two photos will remain forever.

Biography

Brian Mahany

BRIAN MAHANY is a lawyer with a national practice helping victims of fraud get back their hard-earned money. He also helps people and businesses with tax problems and those accused of white-collar crimes. A lawyer of 27 years, Brian previously served as Maine's revenue commissioner, as an assistant attorney general, and as a criminal investigator. In 2008 he was part of the Wesley Snipes defense team. He lives in Milwaukee, Wisconsin.

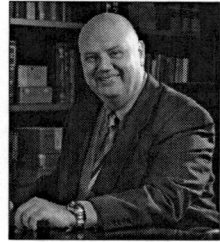

Contact Information

www.mahanyertl.com
brian@mahanyertl.com
414-704-6731

Chapter 14

Engineer Your Success

by Julie Eversole

*M*ost people consider Donald Trump to be a successful businessman. He has big dreams, big successes, and big failures, too. He started in business thinking big. While still in college, he made a $6 million profit on his first construction project, and his net worth is currently reported to be about $2 billion. He has had huge ups and downs along the way. Some of the companies he has owned have declared bankruptcy for hundreds of millions of dollars. And yet, plenty of people are willing to loan Donald Trump money because they believe in his ability to succeed. They know he will always get up again to fight another day. They believe him when he says he will never quit pursuing his dreams and goals. Because of that, he has achieved success and will continue to do so.

Most people don't work business deals as big as Donald Trump's. But that doesn't mean they can't be successful. Success is personal and changes over time. To achieve success, we must translate our dreams into goals. We achieve what we believe we can do. Therefore, we must believe, completely, that success, with all its ups and downs, is worth whatever struggle we encounter along the way.

Define Success for Yourself

Success is defined by each of us based on our perspective at that point in our lives. Success for you is what you define it to be. For example, someone may define success as earning $1 million, but another person may require much more or much less money to consider himself successful. Some may define success as being able to stay home with their young or school-aged children without having to work outside the home. Others may define success differently, such as with relationships or health criteria. Yet another person may consider himself successful because he weighs the same now as he did 20 years ago.

Most people believe someone with a professional degree—that is, a doctor, dentist, veterinarian, lawyer—is successful, as early as on their graduation day, even without knowing their professional accomplishments. They recognize that even with no professional experience, recent graduates have accomplished something exceptional. This measure of success is typically just a milestone in a lifetime of accomplishments. Although most people would consider a new doctor a success, do you think the doctor would end his quest for success at this point? Most do not. Due to differing perspectives, some people may consider the professional a success long before the professional sees himself that way.

For most graduates, graduation is a milestone, or the beginning of a quest for career or financial success. Most people who have just graduated would probably insist they have taken only the first step toward their dreams. In reality, each step of our lives is a potential success marker. The pursuit of success continues our entire lives. Establishing goals and dreams throughout our lives may help achieve success, but celebrating our achievements leads to even greater accomplishments.

The most important key to success is to define it for yourself. Then, establish and work toward goals to reach it. Your success is up to you. When I was working on my bachelor's degree in engineering, I set a goal to graduate with honors. I researched the minimum grade point average (GPA) required and graduated with precisely that GPA. I didn't have a single extra point to spare. I wonder what would have happened if I had set my sights higher? On the other hand, I know for sure that I wouldn't have graduated with honors if I had not calculated exactly what grade I needed in each course and worked to earn those grades.

Set Specific Goals

Goals should be specific, measureable, achievable, and relevant within a set timeframe. Goals should be written to make them real and to help you stay focused on them. Next, determine exactly what is required to reach that goal. This includes determining resources, timelines, and effort needed. Then, divide the tasks required into manageable steps that will culminate in goal achievement. People should have lifetime goals, mid-term goals, and short-term goals. The short-term and mid-term goals should logically lead to the achievement of the lifetime goals.

Let's say you want to save a million dollars by the time you retire in 35 years. To determine how to accomplish this, you need to break the goal into manageable chunks. Determine the amount needed each month to reach that goal. With a monthly investment of $435 at 8%, which has been the average rate of return of the stock market for the past 81 years, you would have $1 million in 35 years. Saving $435 per month, then, would become the short-term goal to ensure you achieve the overall goal of saving $1 million. If desired, it could be broken down into weekly or even daily goals.

Follow Your Own Dreams

You cannot adopt anyone else's dreams as your own. If you do, you cannot expect to be anything but mediocre. People who became lawyers, doctors, or teachers because that was what their parents wanted for them experience no pleasure and little success in their careers. If it isn't your dream or passion, your heart will not be in it. Make your dreams your own. Define them yourself and pursue them with passion.

I spent more than 20 years in the Air Force. I'm a retired Air Force engineer. Although I set and attained goals on the job, I never purposefully set personal goals while I was in the military. Specifically, I never strived to attain a certain rank. When I first entered the military as an enlisted person, however, I overheard another recruit say she wanted to become a major because her father had retired as a major. You might have guessed that I retired as a major. Apparently, I had subconsciously adopted her goal since I had set none of my own.

Without goals you may be working on everything and yet be heading nowhere. It is as though you are shooting at targets in a room without knowing their location. Eventually, you might get lucky and hit one; however, the chances are slim that you will succeed without wasting precious time and resources. Without a specific target, how likely is it that you will hit the one you most want to reach? Success is much more attainable if you know where you are going and focus your time and resources on that target.

Celebrate Success

To help us achieve future goals, we should recognize and celebrate each success as it occurs. When you've saved $435 per month for a year, or for 10 years, celebrate it. When you graduate from high school, celebrate your achievement. When you've paid off your home mortgage, celebrate it. Although most people would like to have no mortgage, many people never set that as a goal, so they never achieve it. Your celebration of each success will result in positive feedback to you. As you see results from achieving short-term goals, you will be more inclined to set mid-term goals and believe that you can achieve them. This positive feedback creates a positive self image in your brain. What you believe, you can achieve.

Many of us need to reprogram our brains to truly believe we are capable of achieving our dreams. We sometimes have to change our thinking to believe we even deserve to reach our dreams. Allow yourself to fully consider and appreciate each achievement, and then strive to improve from there. Previous achievement makes us believe that future achievement is possible. We have to believe our future success is possible before it can become a reality.

Risk Failure to Achieve True Success

Realize that failure may be a necessary part of success. Consider Babe Ruth, the Baseball Hall of Famer. He simultaneously held the Major League Baseball records for the most strike-outs *and* for the most home runs. That may be because he always strived to hit a home run. He was willing to attempt the best (a home run) at the risk of failure (striking out). However, it is unlikely that Babe Ruth looked at a strike-out as failure. He probably just saw it as an inevitable aspect of hitting home runs. Likewise, it is unlikely that anyone would consider him a failure in baseball even though he held the record for most strike-outs. Most likely, if Babe Ruth had been content with mediocrity, by going for a hit rather than a home run, we probably wouldn't even know his name today.

Maintain Balance in Your Life

Our goals should balance all aspects of our lives—financial, spiritual, social, family, mental, physical, and emotional. What happiness will there be with success in one area of our life if it results in no time for anything else? Many people trade time for money; then they realize the desired success didn't bring them the happiness they expected. Specifically, some people may define success for themselves as earning a particular income. Once they succeed at earning that amount, sometimes they find they don't have time to enjoy the money, or their personal lives have suffered in the process. Perhaps they missed all their children's activities, or maybe their spouse left them due to lack of companionship. Strive for balance so that you can fully embrace and appreciate the successes you achieve. This will ensure your accomplishments are worth the struggle.

Continue Improving

Once you achieve your desired success, you should be prepared to incrementally improve on that for the rest of your life. If you are content with where you are, you will not strive to improve, and therefore, you will not achieve excellence. Likewise, set new goals throughout your life. Don't let any success achieved be the best you ever do. Keep working to improve on your achievements. Admittedly, the improvement may be minute, but continuing to improve incrementally will take you toward excellence. You will also be more likely to keep the success you have attained and to get better and achieve more.

Focus on Your Goals

For everything you do, ask yourself: Will this take me one step closer to reaching my goals, or will it take me away from my goals? If it will not help you with your goals, then consider not doing that activity. A major cause of unmet dreams is broken focus. Keep your eye on the target. Every step you take should get you closer not further from it.

There is a price to pay to achieve any worthy goal. Stay focused on the goal and how great the future will be once you achieve it. Never focus on the price to be paid. You can pay the price in tiny increments and reach the goal. You just have to be disciplined enough to do that. Keep in mind that simple disciplines repeated daily will help you achieve your goals. Problems will occur in anything worth doing, but never let your problems grow to the point where they become bigger than your dream. Stay focused on the goal while you work out the solutions to the problems. Challenges will make you stronger and will make reaching the goal that much more fulfilling.

Pursue Your Dreams with Passion

Make your goals lofty and what you truly desire. Donald Trump said, "If you're going to be thinking anyway, you might as well think big." Set your goals; then commit to reaching them. Never, ever, ever give up on your dreams! Never let there be any doubt about what you want: not in your mind, or in anyone else's. Once you have set your life-time goals, don't ever give up on them, for if you do, you will certainly fail to reach them. The British abolitionist, Sir Thomas Foxwell Buxton, wrote, "With ordinary talent and extraordinary perseverance, all things are attainable." Perseverance is necessary to achieve anything worth having. Realize that it will not be easy to reach your goals; and if it is, you haven't set your goals high enough. Don't ever give up on your dreams no matter how out of reach they seem. Achieving success is not easy; but if you have set your goals on what you truly want, you will find a way to get there. Success is absolutely worth it.

Biography
Julie Eversole

JULIE EVERSOLE, an entrepreneur in the largest industry in the world, travel, helps people achieve their personal and financial goals. As an Air Force engineer, she managed construction projects totaling nearly $1 billion in 15 countries. She oversaw reconstruction in war-torn Bosnia working for the special assistant to the president of the United States and for World Bank. After military retirement, she volunteered thousands of hours for her local school district, the Red Cross, and her church. For over 10 years she has been a consultant to nonprofit organizations. She has a bachelor of industrial engineering degree from Georgia Tech and a master of science in systems management from the University of Southern California.

Contact Information

www.EversoleTravel.com
Julie@EversoleTravel.com

Chapter 15

On Our Journey as Liberating Leaders

by Cheri Avery Black

Place of Power

I'm lying in the meadow, basking in the sunshine, surrounded by tall grass, wildflowers, and warm sweet smells. In the blue sky, puffy white clouds change shape, exciting my imagination.

This vivid memory from my Kansas childhood is my Place of Power, where I am free, loved, and at one with the universal source. There, I am unique, all-powerful me.

In moments when I feel overwhelmed, scattered, or just off track, this vision inspires me to regain strength and clarity. When I'm feeling appreciated, energized, and even challenged , it urges me express gratitude and renewal.

We each have our way to feel the powerful oneness with the universal energy, our God-force, our source. Our Place of Power helps connect us to this source of all we need to be successful and to lead. When we emotionalize clearly our desires and dreams, our Why, and give up the How to our source, results flow effortlessly to and through us.

Many have forgotten about their source as it is buried by layers of fears and limiting beliefs. Those wanting more from life dig down through this layered muck. We are helped by the tools of **Choice**, **Happiness**, **Energy**, **Responsibility** and **Inner** fortitude. At first, these tools may be dull, but by using them consistently, sharpening and polishing them with lifelong personal development, they become tools of liberation. As we uncover our source, we can attract a magnificent life of fulfillment and freedom for ourselves and others we touch.

Choice

Decisive leaders choose quickly, cutting off uncertainty by focusing on compelling dreams. At times in our journey, our awareness of how powerful we are may be blurred. As our source is cleared, we choose to transform this muck of failure into fertilizer for success.

I sat for hours without moving or feeling anything. My spirit was numb. I had started to leave to spend a weekend with friends when the boyfriend called me back into the house. My submission was deeper than stepping over the threshold. I dropped into a pit of resignation, doomed to be controlled by another.

The phone rang while the boyfriend was asleep. Carrie urged me to come over. Like a zombie, I made my way to the car. I tried to press on the accelerator to leave my prison. I couldn't. The weight of my nothingness was too great.

Far inside I heard my parents from my childhood, "You can do anything you set your mind to. We love you." This time the car moved.

Carrie and other friends confronted me to stop playing the victim and choose to live the beautiful life I had. They uplifted me with reminders of my abilities and accomplishments and of my family and friends. I realized that even those who grow up in a strong, loving "Ozzie and Harriet" home, like me, can have their power of choice blindsided and fall into blaming others for their plight.

I chose to face the boyfriend by myself. I had told him many times to leave. Now I knew it wasn't about him, but about the clarity of my intention. This time I said with conviction, "Mountain, Move," This time he left.

Happiness

Positive leaders exude happiness, attracting others who want this too. Our contagious smiles come from discovering who we are and acting in congruence with that awareness.

Each of us is an individual expression of the God-force. My parents had instructed me, "Your life is God's gift to you. What you do with it is your gift to God." When we are true to our uniqueness, we add the most value to others and know that we have given life our best. Happiness results when we are filled with gratitude, with our hearts open to receive blessings. As we gratefully listen to our source no matter what, our hearts begin receiving. For me, despite the obstacles, my two biggest dreams intertwined to bring both to life: finding the love of my life, and owning a guest home in Jamaica. To attract my husband I started speaking the qualities I most desired in him. During that time, I went to Jamaica to find my guest home.

"Go to the countryside," a voice inside me was relentless. My vacation partner took me from my favorite beach to visit a small rural town nestled in the mountains. I immediately knew the man

I met there would be my husband. He vibrated those qualities I had spoken - one who totally adored me, was spiritually centered and would create an attractive home life for us. His two small boys were my bonus.

My caring friends cried, "Listen, the universe is telling you No." It seemed so. The Jamaican postal service went on strike, preventing visa forms from arriving. The U.S. government closed down embassies for five weeks, not once, but twice. The rules changed about who could get a visa, when.

These obstacles and more tested our resolve, but we forged through them and married, raising our boys to be first in their family to graduate college.

Financial setbacks caused friends to strongly advise that my dream home was unrealistic. Our source made a way. My husband refined his building skills, and with a few other miracles, our completed mountaintop guest home now stands as a beautiful symbol of the elevated life of abundance we're attracting.

I have not always accepted abundance, believing that wealthy people were inevitably exploitative, greedy, and miserable. This is one of the beliefs that keep many locked in poverty and scarcity mentalities, with sabotaging thoughts of jealousy, hate, unworthiness, money as anti-spiritual, and a fixation on 'lack of' rather than the possibilities. 'Lack vs. abundance' sounds like 'I can't afford it' vs. 'I'm making a way to get it.'

The verse "I have come that they may have life and have it abundantly" (John 10:10) became my anecdote liberating me from my resistance to blessings. I had misinterpreted the acceptance of blessings as a statement that I was superior. The abundant life was blocked so couldn't release me from the scramble just to meet physical needs. Liberation has aligned me with successful people who have attracted abundance not by exploitation but by liberating others to achieve their dreams.

Energy

Enthusiastic leaders strive for vibrant well-being. Enthusiasm is a powerful emotion of energy. The word's Greek root is *en theos*, the God within, the universal energy source.

To keep that source flowing through us, we must protect and nurture our health—physical, mental, emotional, and spiritual.

Stressful nonstop hard work, an expectation in this workaholic country, is unhealthy causing death and dis-ease. The body needs time to cleanse, recover and rejuvenate. Poor health can be all consuming and distract us from our purpose.

> *My body was tortured by arthritis. I could barely walk or write. I tried Western medicine to no avail. Friends surrounded me with sympathy.*
>
> *A Buddhist friend, Nguyen, came to me with a different message: "You're twice lucky. First, you've known little adversity; now you've been blessed to empathize with the suffering most of the world is experiencing." I would appreciate that later; now I needed the second lucky to bring me relief.*
>
> *"This is a lifestyle choice. Stop working long hours, enjoy family and friends, meditate, move with Tai Chi, become a vegetarian, drink water, and breathe deeply."*
>
> *I applied this choice and my misery thankfully disappeared.*

Since experiencing my dis-ease crisis, I remind myself, with a metaphor from airline flights, to put my oxygen mask (health) on first, before attempting to help others. Earlier, I had gained a lot of knowledge about health and neglected to apply it. True power is in the application.

Responsibility

Effective leaders accept 100% responsibility for our lives. We don't blame others or our circumstances. We don't engage in wishful waiting for someone to lead us. We set goals, strategize, and take action.

The universe has a sense of humor. It likes to challenge us when we're on top of the world, even when we're at the bottom. It helps to remember: "Only when it's dark can we see the stars." (MLK Jr.)

> *The new director of the Philadelphia Office of Mental Health (POMH) stripped away my title and staff after 15 years as an outstanding manager. Even men on the executive team came out of the director's office crying.*
>
> *I faced my fear and, without crumbling, documented to him why I should be reinstated. I still see his "steely gray eyes," like the villains in romance novels. He refused, outraged at my audacity.*
>
> *I thought of Dostoyevsky, "Only by self-respect will you compel others to respect you." I resolved to continue doing my best.*
>
> *Within months, the director created a deputy director position and elevated me to fill it. Honors followed from the U.S. Postal Service "For Accomplished Women in Business," Lutheran Children and Family "For Services to Women," the PRIME Institute "For Excellence in Multicultural Leadership," Abington Memorial Hospital "For leading their journey toward inclusion," and a book dedication by The Multicultural Resource Center. These benchmarks were attracted by the person I was becoming with my commitment to serve others.*

Inner Fortitude

Courageous leaders endure, facing whatever adversity arises. To conquer fear, we take action. By going to our limits in key areas, we

126

can expand ourselves in other areas. When we risk nothing, we risk even more. One peak experience solidified the focus and resolve I use to persevere:

> *Feeling trapped in the intimidating Class 5 Zambezi River in Africa, I was on my first whitewater rafting trip. The guide instructed us before each of the raging rapids. One instruction shook my attention. "If you fall out, don't swim to the bank. See the crocodiles waiting for you!"*
>
> *I swore with every fiber of my being that I was not falling out. In amazement I later watched the trip video. My whole body repeatedly bounced high in the air, but my grasp held tightly on the safety rope below.*
>
> *Now, when facing difficulties, I just call on my crocodile allies.*

Inner fortitude also means having backup plans and adjusting our course as needed, anticipating and appreciating the ups and downs on our journey. When the rug is pulled out from under us, we get back up, stronger.

> *The next director came to POMH, and I was on the outs again. Taking a cue from the Br'er Rabbit fable, I got her to "throw" me into the university-based Multicultural Training and Research Institute (now PRIME) as the director.*
>
> *After years of excellent results and national recognition, another POMH executive came. Without warning, she terminated the Institute's contract with my salary, benefits, and free college tuition for our sons.*
>
> *Fortunately, I was able to survive the financial shock with two plan B businesses that are now my plan A. With WorldVentures, we market the first travel-based financial social network and Dreamtrips benefits to promote business and employee health. Through The Citizenre Corporation, we contribute to*

environmental health through residential rental of solar panels.
Both companies reward us exponentially the more people we help,
reflecting the core ingredient of success.

Many, like me, have been saved through having multiple streams
of income and inspiration to generate stability in our lives so that we
have the time and energy to focus on our purpose.

We Are the Place of Power

Few are willing to do what it takes to attract the success of a fulfilled
life. Join me with gratitude, claim your dreams and uncover your source
so the results desired stream into and through us to help others.

Imagine celebrating the extreme joy of fulfilling your wildest
dreams. Then force yourself to feel the extreme pain of a lifetime of
unfulfilled dreams. When you feel intensely from the depths of your
source that remaining in your 'safe' bud is more painful than the risk
it takes to blossom then you are on our journey.

The world is calling out from the darkness and we have appeared,
radiating love's powerful light. We *are* the liberating leaders others are
looking for.

Biography

Cheri Avery Black

CHERI AVERY BLACK is a joyful friend, coach, team builder, mentor, trainer, speaker, author, and humanitarian. She takes pleasure helping others achieve their dreams with referral marketing. As part of her environmental commitment, she promotes renewable energy, focusing on residential rental of solar panels for affordable clean generation of electricity. She markets travel products for family and financial well-being, as vacation benefits for employee health and wellness, and as fun fund generation for nonprofits.

Cheri is a former government executive, university administrator, and professor, and she continues to direct the PRIME Institute (Partners Reaching to Improve Multicultural Effectiveness) She and her husband reside in Philadelphia, where they raised their two boys. They enjoy spending time with friends and family in the Midwest, at their guest home in Montego Bay, and at other points around the world.

The author is donating a portion of her proceeds to the Manifest Foundation, the Ewomennetwork Foundation, SoZo Sisters, Prison Visitation and Support, the Land Institute, the Columbia Support Network, and the PRIME Institute.

Contact Information

www.travelpowur.com
www.energypowur.info
Cblack.4powur@gmail.com
215-882-4351

Chapter 16

Create the Future You Desire
MANAGE TOWARD
YOUR BEST POSSIBLE OUTCOME

by Dr. Sandra M. Matheson

I am most at home on the farm. My earliest memories include spending time in the barn, exploring the nearby woods, playing with my pets, and being out with the cattle. I find both joy and peace lying in green grass looking up at the blue sky or observing the cattle graze on a summer day. After years of watching newborn animals come into the world and take their first awkward steps, the experience is no less impactful. And, as there is life on the farm, there is also death. I have shed many a tear over the loss of a newborn that would never grow up or an aged pet as it took its last breath. It is a glorious circle of life. As a farmer, I feel it is both a great responsibility and an honor to take care of the animals, feed the people, and heal the land. These experiences are the core of my being. They have shaped who I am today. I have always been a farmer, and I expect I always will be.

It was evident early on that I was a nurturer, teacher, explorer, and a healer. What I desire most is to explore what marvelous things nature and man have created, treat all living things with compassion and respect, heal the earth through sustainable agriculture practices, help people reach their full potential, and have a positive impact on the world.

It may seem like I've had an idyllic life, but it wasn't always easy. I was a bit of a dreamer and looked at things differently than most people. I was artistic and creative. Unfortunately, my penmanship was somewhat "creative" as well. I vividly recall being told in grade school by a counselor that because I was left handed with poor handwriting, I would never graduate from high school nor succeed in anything. I would be a "failure in life."

As you can imagine, that experience made a profound an impression on me! However, being the stubborn optimist and creative thinker that I was, those comments reinforced that I was meant to be some kind of doctor. In that moment, I vowed to prove his predictions wrong. I graduated from high school as the valedictorian and went on to earn my doctor of veterinary medicine degree.

Although I've had many wonderful successes in my life, the poisonous seed of self-doubt planted by that school counselor sprouted time and time again. It manifested as a lack of self-confidence and frequently hindered my progress. It is something that I still must actively prune back so I may continue to move toward my dreams. My self-doubt has been one of my biggest roadblocks to success.

I loved veterinary medicine, but after 16 years of practice, I became ill from the disinfectants. It was a quick end to a lifelong dream and a rewarding career. I was angry and bitter at first. Our marriage was troubled. We were in debt. That seed of self-doubt, poor self-esteem, poverty mentality, and lack of confidence evolved into self-sabotage.

I wanted to be successful but couldn't find the courage to follow through. I didn't like where I was, but I couldn't be anywhere else.

Fortunately, a mentor shared this timely insight: "Wherever you are right now, you are there because you choose to be." I was incensed! I didn't choose to be unhappy, in debt, and unemployed. But in the midst of my internal ranting, I realized it was true. It's said that "the devil you know is better than the devil you don't know." I was in that state because of my poor decisions, fear, and inaction.

But it took another mentor before the lesson solidified. One day as I lamented my troubles and asked God, "Why me and what do I do now?" he gave me a simple answer. I knew at that moment I was meant to do something different in my life. In fact, with more free time, my children and I were finally able to do many things we had wanted to do for a long time. The life change led to new experiences we didn't even imagine. In that moment, I began to take responsibility for my life and my future. I am now a documentary filmmaker. I love filmmaking as much as I love farming. It is another gift I can share with the world.

In my quest for success, I learned the difference between a problem and an opportunity. It's not so much what happens in life, but how one responds that matters. The choice is to see it as a problem or embrace it as an opportunity to learn from and move forward. I only wish I had learned this earlier!

When self-doubt creeps up on me, I remind myself that I am successful, intelligent, and worthy. Daily affirmations help me move from the negative attitude to the positive. Fear used to keep me from growing. My college adviser, Dr. Raymond Wright, told me that overcoming fear and stepping out of one's comfort zone to embrace a new challenge builds character. I am forever grateful to him for those words. I now see my anxiety and fear as the precursor to new opportunity, and I welcome it.

The key to success for me and for anyone is to believe that it is possible and that we are worthy of it. Unless we can overcome our doubt, it is unlikely we can accomplish what we desire. Often, the greatest obstacle to success is our unconscious belief that we don't deserve good things to happen to us.

When we can overcome that obstacle, we can take the next big step toward our dreams: Acting on them. We have to actively create the future we desire. Your dream won't come true simply by wishing and doing nothing. You must create an effective plan and take action.

Here are some of the steps that have helped me achieve my dreams:

1. **The first step to success is to know where you want to be.** I was fortunate to be introduced to a decision-making process called Holistic Management, developed by Allan Savory. It transformed my way of thinking, making decisions, managing business, and living life. It is based on a comprehensive "holistic-goal"—the future we seek to create. This differs from ordinary goals that can pull us in conflicting directions. A holisticgoal leads to only one place—our desired future.

   Part of where you want to be involves assessing where you are and how you got there so that your new goal takes you down a different path. There's the old saying, "Keep on doing what you're doing and you'll keep on getting what you're getting." Taking the same path leads to the same destination.

2. **The second step is to write it down.** This would seem easy but is often difficult for many people. A single holisticgoal on paper is worth 20 in one's head. The simple act of writing it down means the likelihood of achieving it is much higher than if it is not.

   First review on paper what you bring with you. These may be skills, experiences, knowledge, and any resources that can help you along your new path. Be clear about what you actually manage vs. what you simply influence and who makes the decisions in your life or business. This reminds you what you have to work with and creates clarity.

The core of the holisticgoal reflects one's principles and values. I ask myself, "How would I want my life to be right now if I could have it any way? Why do I want this? What does it mean to me? What must I produce to create and sustain that quality of life? What must my land, business, and other resources look like in order to support the future I desire?" I write in the present tense. Doing so allows me to feel it, believe it, and experience it in the here and now. Posting the holisticgoal where it can be seen will keep it ever-present in my thoughts.

3. **Next, create possible action plans along with timelines.** The timeline allows a plan to be completed in doable steps and provides accountability.

4. **Then test your plans.** We cannot assume that our proposed plans are correct just because we thought of them! Testing the planned action is necessary to determine if it will lead toward the desired outcome – the holisticgoal. If not, revise your plan or create a new one. Testing decisions has saved me countless dollars and hours.

5. **Monitor the process.** Just because a decision was tested doesn't mean it actually turns out as planned. Monitoring is very important. A simple review will indicate if the plan is leading toward success or away from it. Look for the *earliest* possible indicator that things are going awry, and then get back to right path.

6. Revise and adapt your plans to change. Life sometimes gets in the way. People change, and things get complicated. Revise both your holistic goal and your action plans as circumstances change.

One aspect of my holistic goal is to achieve my desired quality of life and keep an optimum balance among relationships, finances, and the environment. It's the "triple bottom line" that defines sustainability. All the riches and clout in the world mean very little if people and the environment are damaged in the process of obtaining them.

However, above that is a greater definition of success. In the end, I want to know that I've made a positive difference in the world. Whether in many small ways or in a few big ways, that is the legacy I wish to leave.

Biography

Dr. Sandra M. Matheson

DR. SANDRA MATHESON is a lifelong rancher and writer, and a retired veterinarian in beautiful Washington State. As a consensus facilitator, as well as a certified educator and accredited associate consultant in holistic management, she has worked with many people from the United States and abroad to help them move toward the future they desire. In addition to ranching, Sandra's other passion is filmmaking. She is the co-owner of Raincrow Film LLC, creating impactful documentary films in the areas of innovation, sustainability, agriculture, society, and culture. Dr. Matheson also serves as the president for Managing Change Northwest and the Washington Simmental Association.

Contact Information

www.createthefutureyoudesire.com
www.raincrowfilm.com
www.mathesonfarms.com
360-220-5103

Chapter 17

Living Intrepidly

by Demi Karpouzos

For most of my adult life, I struggled to find what my purpose was. Sadly, I didn't know what I was passionate about. I'd stifled my emotions for so long that I'd forgotten what brought me joy. Being the quintessential people pleaser, I was too busy trying to figure out what would make other people happy that I didn't have time to discover what made me happy. Mediocrity was my status quo for the longest time. But then a camping trip with a friend set the stage for where I would end up, giving me a glimpse of what I was capable of.

In high school, camping trips consisted of pulling the car up to the campsite, pitching a tent, and sitting around the fire talking. So when my friend Paul approached me to go on a "real" camping trip, where we would have to hike to our site, I accepted the challenge. This trip would become a metaphor for life.

I began with great excitement: some trepidation, but more excitement. That morning I threw together a few things I thought we would need on our trip. A few weeks prior, Paul had asked if I had a backpack and I had told him that I did. The morning of the trip, when he came to pick me up, he looked incredulously at what I had slung over my shoulder. I discovered that a backpack and a knapsack are not the same thing. Not only had I thrown things together the morning of the trip instead of properly preparing ahead of time, but I had made the grave error of not knowing what I didn't know. I was ill prepared because I hadn't done my due diligence, and this would prove to make our trip more arduous than it needed to be.

We hiked for approximately 14 kilometers to get to our campsite. The hike was tiring not only because of the distance but because we had to carry so many bags in our hands (my knapsack could only hold so much). We were both exhausted. We pitched our tent, found a tree with a high branch to throw our food over so that bears wouldn't invade our site, and I got ready for sleep. In the middle of the night, I was awakened to Paul yelling that the tent was flooded and we'd have to pack up and head back. It was 3 a.m., I was still exhausted, and it was pouring rain. The thought of having to hike back 14 kilometers in the dark and in the pouring rain broke my spirit. I didn't know how I was going to make it. The first step was the hardest, but once we started moving, it wasn't so bad. I would choose a tree or a rock in the distance to be my milestone marker. I broke it up into steps (a lot of steps).

It seemed like we had been walking forever, and I started to give up. It didn't look like we were nearing the end, and I was tired, hungry, angry, and wet. I didn't think I had another step left in me. Yet every time I wanted to give up, I remembered all the other times I had given up on myself; I didn't want to be this person anymore. And with this new resolve, I found I had another step in me, and another, and another. Before I knew it, I saw the truck, and I can tell you without any shame that it brought tears to my eyes. Sure, I was exhausted, and I was now starting to feel a cold coming on, but the tears were not just tears of relief. My tears were for my epiphany. I was now becoming aware of how small I had been living my life because I hadn't thought I was worthy or that I had what it took to live a brilliant life. I now saw my accountability for the position that I found myself in, and I knew it didn't mean that I had to keep making the same choices.

This small test of my will bolstered my confidence, and I was ready to test myself again. And I did. I quit smoking. I used the same method of making a promise to myself (or what some would call a goal), asking myself why I was making this promise, preparing, and breaking it down into smaller steps. Initially I broke it down minute by minute, and then when I had a little time under my belt, it became day by day, and at the 21-day mark, I knew I had begun to form a new habit; it was no longer a battle with an old way of thinking. I wondered if this would work for purchasing my first home. Purchasing real estate investment properties? Purchasing stocks? Starting a business? I discovered that the answer was a resounding *Yes*!

Lofty goals are great, but be aware of how you define success. I thought by earning a lot of money, driving a luxury car, and owning a condo on the lake, I'd feel successful. Don't get me wrong, I very much enjoyed what I had acquired, but my job was just a job, and like most people, I dreaded Mondays and looked forward to Fridays. When I'm asked the question now, I can truthfully say that when you're engaged in something you enjoy, you become the person you need to become to get to the destination of whatever your goal is, whether it be making a lot of money, having a lot of toys, traveling, and so forth—to me, that is success. Do what you love, take chances, live fully, and when you can look back on your life and you don't utter "I wish I would have," know that you have succeeded.

The single most important key in achieving success is persistent action. Thomas Edison "failed" countless times with his inventions before achieving his desired result. Marry persistent action with passion and knowledge.

What can you do to make persistent action part of your game plan? I challenge you to find what you're passionate about and then prepare by becoming as informed as you need to be to take the *first* step. Trust that opportunities will arise and people will show up when you need to take the next step. Abraham Lincoln said that if he had six hours to chop down a tree, he would spend the first hour sharpening his knife. That's all you need to do. Know what your goal is, why you want to achieve it, map it out, prepare for the first step, and then take action!

You will probably encounter some roadblocks. This is where persistent action is crucial. Some of the roadblocks I've experienced on my journey have been self-doubt, insecurity, lack of self-worth, and money identification. When making choices with this frame of mind, I soon discovered (well, not so soon) that the results were far from good and that there was definitely a distinct pattern that brought about my less-than-desirable outcomes. Because I was aware of my hurdles, I knew that I needed to take persistent action at every turn. I started devouring books. I was relentless in my learning (and I still am). I read biographies for inspiration. I read self-help books to become more self-aware and to do the inner work necessary to rewrite my internal dialogue, where my limiting beliefs lived. I read investment books to learn how to do what I wanted to do to get to where I wanted to go. I attended seminars for motivation—but I warn you not to become an information junky. I discovered that some people went from seminar to seminar and never took action, or if they did take action, they'd allow their motivation to dwindle and then have to go to the next seminar to get hyped up again. Let this not be you.

I saw some great progress in my life, but there were still a few trigger points I realized would keep me stuck. As a result, I hired a coach. She not only held me accountable but more importantly, she was able to give me feedback from a different perspective. For the first time I saw where I was sabotaging myself and how to align my intentions and my actions. Hiring my own coach also helped me to squash any doubts I might have had regarding the value of my service as a coach. I understood that a good coach will get you to your goals quicker and more efficiently than if you try to do it on your own.

They say that we overestimate what we can do in a year and underestimate what we can do in five years. Remember that the time will go by regardless, so you might as well work toward something you love so that five years from now, you won't regret not having done something different with yourself. Lead your life and, regardless of what your position is in this world, you can be a great leader. Great leaders inspire people to do better and to be better. Great leaders do the things that most people aren't willing to do, even though they might not like doing it either. They have the discipline to do what's important. They consistently express their absolute best. Great leaders inspire and influence by their example each person they meet. They treat everyone with respect, appreciation, and kindness, knowing that we are all connected and that when you give the best of yourself, you get the best out of others. Leadership isn't about dictatorship. It's about going out on a limb and inspiring others to do the same.

"Life begins at the end of your comfort zone." You need to trust that it isn't coincidence that you're reading this book. You are hungry for something better, something greater. Take a chance . . . live boldly . . . and you'll realize what it feels like to be fully alive.

To get out of your comfort zone, it helps to find a mentor who has done the same. Napoleon Hill's book *Think and Grow Rich* has been a great inspiration for me. I am blessed because I have had several mentors in my life. I sought out people who were where I wanted to be. Some were several steps ahead of me, and some were years ahead. I found most of them in the books that lined my shelves. Find a mentor and remember that the only difference between you and that person is just a step. Isn't it time you started living intrepidly?

Biography

Demi Karpouzos

DEMI KARPOUZOS is a certified success coach. She also has real estate investment certifications and has applied her knowledge to create a portfolio with several investment properties. Demi is a humanitarian, and she's had the great honor and pleasure of traveling to Africa on more than one occasion. She is a dream chaser, a limiting belief conqueror, and a goal achiever.

Contact Information

www.strategicalcoaching.com
Demi@strategicalcoaching.com

Chapter 18

17 Ways To Attract Freedom

by Dr. Ken Onu

If you do for a short time what most people won't do for a short time, you will have for a lifetime of what most people can't have for a lifetime.

My name is Dr. Ken, and I want to thank you for taking time out of your busy life to read this chapter. I'm happy and excited that you're reading this book because you're doing something that the majority of people never do—investing in yourself.

I wear many hats. I am the CEO and founder of Attract Freedom. Some of you may know me as a motivational speaker, while others know me as a coach, and yet others as an eye surgeon.

What do a motivational speaker, a coach, and an eye surgeon have in common?

Well, when I'm not working on sight, I'm working on vision. As Helen Keller rightly said, "The only thing worse than blindness is having sight but no vision." My mission in life is to help people eradicate possibility blindness. I focus on vision—the inner and outer vision.

I was born in Africa, but from this point on, I may have to disappoint you. My story is unlike many you've heard about so-called successful people.

You're not going to hear that I was born in a homeless shelter. You're not going to hear that we didn't have clothes to wear or that our fridge was always empty. You're not going to hear that I had holes in my socks or in the roof of my house and the rain was falling in.

No, that's not my story.

In fact, I was quite privileged. My dad was a top diplomat in Africa, and I lived a sheltered life, never knowing that I needed anything. I've lived in many countries in the world. I went to various top schools, passed all my exams, went to university, studied medicine, went on to specialize in ophthalmology, became an eye surgeon, and of course started making a good living.

So I did all these things, yet somewhere, somehow I felt empty. It was an uneasy feeling about life. I felt that something was missing. A feeling I could not put my finger on, and I spent my youth mostly in anger. Angry at the world, angry at the pollution out there, at the cutting of the rain forest, the ozone layer, the starving kids around the world, the oppression of blacks, the slave trade, the holocaust, the senseless wars. You name it, I was angry about it.

And most of all, I was angry with myself, because I had that feeling of helplessness. That I could do nothing about it. Just mention something, and I would rant and rave about it for hours and hours. I got myself into so much trouble because of this.

I was suspended several times from school for inciting others to oppose the laws. I felt empty. I felt no one cared. My scatteredness and confusion did not go away. I was always restless, jumping from one thing to another, one business to another, knowing that there was more out there for me than just being a young black man out of Africa with a degree.

And I failed. A lot. I failed at many things even though outwardly I seemed successful. I failed at my marriage. I failed at my other relationships. I failed at being a good parent, at being organized, focused, and purposeful.

Things would go perfectly well for me, and then I would practice self-sabotage. I had several profitable businesses, and things were going very well, but just like everything else in my life, due to lack of focus, those also went into the ground. I was a good doctor with great ideas, but I needed to pay more attention to the details. And then one day I woke up.

I had no choice, I guess. The banks and creditors were calling for their money, and suddenly all my so-called friends disappeared. I looked around and couldn't find anybody exactly when I needed them most.

That's when it hit me like a ton of bricks. The problem was not anything out there. It wasn't the friends, the bad ones or the good ones. It wasn't the banks. There was just one person responsible for all these woes, and that was me. *Me.*

I knew I had to start working on myself if anything was going to change. I knew I could impact the world but did not know how. I read one thing that I will never forget in my life; somebody somewhere said, "You should never die with your fire still inside of you."

I read more—spiritual books, all kinds of books—watched all kinds of films and videos, and traveled to seminars and retreats around the world. I came across books such as *As a Man Thinketh, The Richest Man in Babylon, Atlas Shrugged, Acres of Diamond,* and *Think and Grow Rich* to name a few, and I discovered that what made me angry was inside me. I learned from people like Dr. Wayne Dyer that it's what's inside that drives you. When you squeeze an orange, what do you get? Orange juice. When you squeeze a human being, you get what was already inside of them. If it's anger, then anger comes out. If it's love, then only love comes out.

I learned how our thoughts affect our feelings and ultimately our behaviors and results. Change the thoughts and you change the results.

So I decided I was going to do something about it. I was going to change. I was going to become whole, perfect, strong, and powerful. I was going to become a loving, happy, harmonious, and prosperous individual. Most of all, I was going to practice gratitude and generosity. I started doing these things, and my life changed overnight. I attracted the things I desired in my life. People and events started showing up at the right time just because of my new way of thinking. This is what I want to talk to you about because before you can even start thinking about success, you have to first deal with the mindset you need to attract freedom.

We go to school for 10 to 20 years, and we learn a lot, but the one thing that is never taught in most schools is how to think right and how to be successful. We learn through trial and error. We fail in so many different things, and we think how great it would be if we only had a handbook to life.

We can be successful if we think the right way, because success is like a combination lock: Once you know the numbers and sequence on the lock, you can open it correctly every single time you try to. We must understand that the only thing holding us back from creating our dreams is ourselves. The enemy is "inside of me."

The other thing that holds us back is fear. The fear of rejection, abandonment, failure, the unknown, loss, and even the fear of success.

We have to understand that *fear* is nothing more than an illusion. It is a coward. Confront it and it hides away like the coward it is. How many of us confront fear? It may be difficult, but know that "difficult is only a description for easy things that take a lot of steps to perform." Keep challenging what you fear and it has no choice but to slink away.

*"Do today what others don't,
and you will have tomorrow what others won't."*

My relationships with my friends, family, patients, and business colleagues have improved tremendously. I look and feel healthier. My creativity is on steroids. I take on project after project with uncanny success. How do I do it?

I would like to share with you 17 ways to attract freedom. These principles have worked for me, and I know they can work for you.

17 Ways to Attract Freedom:

1. *Know what you want.* What are you passionate about? What could you do 24/7 without feeling tired or upset? That's what you should be doing. Devise a plan to achieve whatever it is you are after. Practice visualizing your goals and remember to set a deadline. A goal without a deadline is simply a wish.

2. *Believe you can have it.* Believing you can have something starts by believing in yourself. Healthy self-esteem is absolutely necessary to achieve whatever you want in life. Believe it is possible for you. Never let anyone's opinion of you affect your reality.

3. *Surround yourself with like-minded people.* You are the sum total of the five people you hang around with all of the time. Your income also will usually be about the average of the people you spend the most time with.

   My friend Kimm Dougan shared this with me:

   "There are two types of people in your life: *lifters* and *leaners.* Lifters lift you up, inspire, encourage, believe in you, support you, and are always cheering you on. Leaners lean on you, drag you down, are always critical, and see negatives in everything. Soon their fears, limiting beliefs, and worries rub off on you. *Success* or *failure* in life is sometimes determined by the people you hang around. The decision is yours."

4. *Find a mentor who has achieved what you are seeking to achieve.* If you want to be successful, then model successful people.

5. *Exercise daily.* Drink lots of water and eat lots of fruits and vegetables. Read uplifting material.

6. *Accept total responsibility for your life.* Never *ever* blame anyone or anything for situations or events in your life.

7. *Learn how to forgive others, but first of all, learn how to forgive yourself.*

8. *Be happy to serve other people.* Find random ways to put smiles on their faces. Always put a smile on yours. If you give people value, you will receive valuables.

9. *Live in a state of constant confident expectation.* Focus on what you want and not on what you don't want.

10. *Be grateful.* Count all your blessings. Focus on what you already have. Being grateful will affect your attitude, and that in turn will affect your altitude in life.

11. *Watch your thoughts.* Watch the way you talk to yourself (your self-talk). Practice affirmations and journal your thoughts.

12. *Monitor your feelings throughout the day.* Ask yourself: Why am I feeling this way? Observe yourself as if you were watching someone else. That is what we call awareness. When we are aware, we are in control of our choices.

13. *To attract, you have to be attractive, and to attract, you have to act!* If we take action, even if they are small steps, we will eventually accomplish what we set out to do. Consistency is the key.

14. *Learn how to meditate.* Everything in life is created twice: once on the mental plane and finally in "real" life. We spend too much time focusing on "reality." Our reality tells us lots of lies. If we were to focus more on our inner vision, we would astound ourselves at our rate of success.

15. *Ask!* Learn how to ask for what you want. As they say, if you don't ask, the answer is always no.

16. *Remember "failure" is only a lesson.* It is feedback.

17. And finally: *Always seek to WIN!* A good friend once said: W is for "Willing attitude", I is for (Take the) "Initiative," and N is for "Never give up"!

Are you ready to finally be free?

Biography

Dr. Ken Onu

DR. KEN ONU is an eye doctor with a vision—a vision to eradicate possibility blindness. He is an accomplished growth mentor and a dynamic motivational speaker who has helped thousands of people "see beyond the veil" to achieve their full potential.

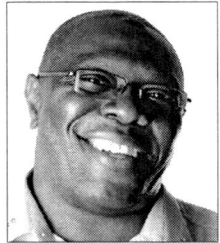

He is the founder of Attract Freedom, a global community of like-minded individuals who help each other attract the type of life they desire. His mission is to "positively change mindsets one person at a time, using the channels of education, seminars, and private coaching."

If you want to learn more ways to attract freedom, be more organized and focused, and conquer fear, visit us at www.attractfreedom. com and sign up for free membership.

Success is not something you chase. . . . You attract it, and Dr. Ken can show you how.

Contact Information

www.attractfreedom.com
drken@attractfreedom.com

Chapter 19

Awakening the Transformational Leader Within

DEVELOPING THE CHARACTERISTICS OF A TRANSFORMATIONAL LEADER

by Wali Mutazammil

Engaging in action learning, being a different observer with new conversations, and evoking consistent archetypes in the domain of the body, emotions and language—that is transformational change, and when you change your inner world in the eye-of-the-heart, that is meaningful change, and you experience your life conditions differently.

What are the characteristics of a transformational leader?

Transformational leaders in the twenty-first century are affecting our world and the quality of life inside and outside the workplace. Noel M. Tichy and Mary Ann Devanna, co-authors of *The Transformational Leader*, through their extensive research and in-depth interviews, discovered common characteristics among transformational leaders throughout global cultures: They are courageous, change agents and leaders, values driven, believers in people, lifelong learners, comfortable with dealing in complexity, and visionaries.

In my own path toward transformational leadership, I have learned the value of these characteristics through my own experiences and used them to facilitate transformation in the lives of others.

Courageous

August 6, 2001, I experienced a courageous awakening after I woke up from a successful surgery that had removed all the cancer from my body. I was inspired to continue my life-learning journey with a vision of becoming a servant for leadership that makes a difference in our world by serving others.

This part of my journey began in 2002, as a student at Georgetown University in Washington, D.C., in my graduate studies leadership coaching certificate course. I had volunteered to be a coachee during our first week of the program in front of my classmates, who were total strangers to me at that time.

I gave my professor permission to facilitate the role as my leadership coach. During the coaching session, I had several "aha" moments. One of them was powerful and left me tearful, and several were quite embarrassing in a public setting. This was my first coaching session and I was willing to go for it, so we continued, and I discovered that I was able to journey into a scared place that I called the "eye-of-the-heart," and it was there that I consciously listened to my soul for the first time ever.

My leadership coach invited me to face head-on a story that for 20 years had kept me living intermittently in resentment. It was a story of blame, guilt, victimization, shame, self-pity, helplessness, and hopelessness, perceptions of not being enough, of being inadequate and Slim's little brother, too short, and a Montgalleon, i.e., growing up on Montgall Street. I was consciously and subconsciously in denial of all the accomplishments I had achieved over the last 20 years. I had been selected as a Harry S Truman Scholar and received invitations to complete my undergraduate degree from Harvard, Stanford, Oxford, Yale, and Georgetown, which I did not accept due to family obligations. The truth is I never realized that it was possible to choose and live a different story. It was through a new self-awareness and conscious efforts, coupled with leadership coaching, that I began to produce extraordinary results as an ordinary person. Through this experience, I was able to acknowledge that those Ivy League universities were still there, and I could choose to go to them anytime I wanted to. My inner voice asked, Can you count what you have achieved and the successes that our world has acknowledged you for since you chose not to accept those scholarly offers? There were too many to count. I had adapted to my situation and excelled. Finally, through this coaching, I could recognize this.

Tip for success: Courage requires being adaptive and embracing interrelated skills.

Change Agent and Leader

I have experienced an awakening as a change agent and leader in identifying and honoring my power, fostering resonance with co-active team members, and inviting emotional activism within individuals, teams, organizations, communities, and nations to lead people to a place where they have never been.

One of my successes as a change agent occurred in 1995. Dr. Ray Blanchard and I in a smart partnership successfully assisted the former prime minister of Malaysia Dr. Mahathir Mohamad and senior government officials in achieving Malaysia's Vision 2020 through transformational learning and transformative work in addressing the human components of transformational change. Since that time, I have been internationally acknowledged for my capacity and abilities to universally apply transformation as a change leader.

Tip for success: Being a genuine change agent and leader means understanding leadership as the art and science of bringing about transformational change.

Values Driven

In 2002, I had an awakening as a values-driven leader through practicing with scientific and innovative tools for building values-driven teams and organizations. One tool was a Values-Based Leadership Wheel that focused on nine principles: choice, integrity, risk taking, honesty, 100% participation, responsibility, smart partnerships, committed actions, and lightness. The Values-Based Leadership Wheel, coupled with the Wheel of Life and a List of Enemies of Learning, will unmask inhibitions to living a balanced, healthier, and more productive lifestyle, rather than striving for a perfect lifestyle, which is not realistic by any standards.

Tip for success: Being an authentic leader requires leading from your values, not from perfection.

Believer in People

In 1994, Dr. Blanchard and I, a former student of his, facilitated transformational learning and transformative work with Malaysia's largest conglomerate Sime Darby Plantation. We agreed that we would speak to the executives' human souls rather than to their traditional cultural beliefs, intellects, and so forth. When individuals are open and willing to learn, something magical happens inside their inner world and they embrace the new body of knowledge.

I designed and facilitated experiential learning modules because people retain and embrace more knowledge through experience than through simply gathering more information. We were effective and successful with our transformational work at Sime Darby Plantation. One executive described our work as "excellent, the best short-term learning program I have ever experienced, way beyond my expectations, changed my worldview."

Tip for success: Believe in yourself and in other people's abilities to transform through experience.

Lifelong Learner

I experience a new awakening as a lifelong learner every day. I see many distinctions and infinite possibilities in our world, which is constantly changing, unpredictable, chaotic environments and complex systems. At the Human Systems Dynamics Institute (HSDI), we are still learning the fundamentals that exist in all systems and developing understanding as well as gratitude for the opportunity to influence patterns in organizational settings. When I am able to see and understand patterns that come from energy, I am able to see what others do not see in complex systems, chaos, and the unspoken. My new eyes, capacity, and abilities in emotional competence enable me to help teams and leaders coping with chaos.

Tip for success: Be a lifelong learner and understand that there is always something new to learn.

Ability to Deal with Complexity, Ambiguity, and Uncertainty

In 1996, I experienced my most painful and blessed awakening ever when I heard that Rasheedah Ni'mat Mutazammil, my daughter, had been innocently murdered while lying in her bed with her three-month-old son in Washington, D.C. Allah (Lord of all Worlds/ The Merciful Redeemer, The Merciful Benefactor) teaches in His Quran that we are to obey the laws of the country where we are living.

As a former law student at the International Islamic University in Malaysia, I remembered my professor and former classmates discussing the story of Prophet Mohammed (Allah's peace be upon him) when one of his daughters was thrown from her horse and died. The innocent man attending her riding was accused of murder by certain people living in Medina and went into hiding, scared for his life. Finally, the townspeople found the man and brought him to Prophet Mohammed (pbuh), who immediately empathized with the man's sadness of being in fear, hiding and living with trauma. The man felt overwhelmed with the hospitality and the personal treatment of Prophet Mohammed (pbuh) and later converted to Islam.

I was, of course, angry and uncomfortable dealing with the complexities of my emotions and psyche, the legal system, and the murderer's lack of remorse. However, having access to a story on how Prophet Mohammed (pbuh) had set an example of the teachings of Allah's Quran in dealing with the most painful experience that any parent could suffer left me pondering. When I received the news about my daughter, I was working as a consultant, providing technical assistance in marketing and media investment campaigns in Ghana and Malaysia. My dear friends in Ghana shared Quranic teachings that were comforting to my heart, psyche, and soul, and a powerful awakening that enabled me to begin to feel comfort in dealing with the complexities of my daughter's murder: (1) Rasheedah is in paradise without judgment because she was innocently murdered. (2) If we as parents accept Allah's will without seeking revenge we are invited to enter paradise behind Rasheedah as a gift from Allah, because He knows the pain and suffering of any parents who are burying their child. (3) Allah loves Rasheedah more than us as parents, and she was entrusted as a gift and a loan to our family and our world for a short time. Amen.

Tip for success: Practicing spirituality can help you learn to deal with complexity, ambiguity, and uncertainty.

Visionary

Our awakenings as visionary leaders and can be contagious in a family, team, community, nation, and worldwide. Currently, I am in joy observing my daughter Asya Mutazammil consciously living her vision passionately as a media consultant. Asya and I had several exchanges of ideas around her feelings and thoughts before her vision was manifested. Our beautiful exchanges were full of uncertainties, and more. For example, the ideas of just doing it, not being in control, spirituality, proper breathing, going for a walk, eating healthy, practicing patience, noticing how it feels not having the answer, identifying your fears, guilt, sadness, how much you're loved, working from a place of joy, compassion with knowledge, skills and abilities you have to offer. What I told her is true for you: "You are the difference that makes the difference in our world," and now is your time to access your future possibilities today.

Tip for success: Visionaries are courageous followers who support healthy leaders and authentic leadership.

What Is Transformational Leadership?

Transformational leadership is channeling the productive fuel of energy in the direction of the integrity of the authentic vision of a leader. The practice of transformational leadership is witnessing a leader demonstrating being first in leading people to experiencing emotional activism and great adventures in their well-being and wellness, coupled with character.

In Human Systems Dynamics (HSD), as HSD professionals, we understand the productive fuel of energy may be moving from transition-to- transformation-to-transcending (or not) given our universe, which is a non-linear system. Also, HSD professionals can see what others do not see, and influence patterns in organizational settings.

I am healthier sharing my gift, capacity, and abilities in serving others, which is the highest calling in our world. I facilitate how-to skills in choosing to discover future possibilities today; accessing permission for engaging and exploring beyond fear; and leading transformation by dancing with passion onward through a lifelong journey in well-being, wellness, and prosperity.

Leadership that doesn't "bring about transformation" in self and others is not leadership. As America's great jazz legends put it, "If it ain't got that swing, it ain't jazz."

Biography

Wali Mutazammil

WALI MUTAZAMMIL is a Harry S Truman Scholar with over 20 years of experience as a transformational leadership consultant. He is internationally acknowledged as a Wellness Recovery Action Plan (WRAP®) facilitator in the wellness profession. Also, he facilitates learning to develop young talent and nurture the soul of communities for healthier patterns and growth. Clients include the United Nations, IBM, Motorola, American Express, Housing Authority of Baltimore City, The Johns Hopkins Health Systems, Royal Bafokeng Economic Board, and Sime Darby Plantation.

Contact Information

info@tdconsortium.com
443-857-5731

Chapter 20

Bouncing Back Successfully from Any Circumstance

by Henry Maltez

How do you successfully bounce back from the circumstances, challenges, and pitfalls of life?

Some of us may have gone through numerous difficulties in the past year. How do we *release* those thoughts that no longer serve and support us and others? No matter what happened, can we look at our circumstances with a *renewed* point of view? Is it possible that every situation we experience is part of life's lessons and blessings that we are meant to learn and share? Can we continue to evolve with these lessons and gifts we receive, and use them to support and contribute to others?

With a new focus and appreciation, is it possible to *return,* or "bounce back," with a new commitment to take the actions necessary to selflessly build the life and community we dream of?

For the purposes of this chapter, I am sharing two real-life accounts and some profound personal experiences and lessons that have supported me in having great personal and professional success this past year.

My first story begins on September 10, 2009, when I was informed that my mother was sick and possibly dying of cancer at a local hospital. I had a very poor relationship with my mother, and we had not spoken for almost a year. I arrived at the hospital and her doctor told me that she had stomach cancer and that it would be difficult to treat because it had spread to her liver. In addition, she was fighting an infection that kept them from providing any possible treatments, not even for her pain. The cancer could have been slowed if only she had sought treatment and dealt with the warning signs sooner.

I am sharing this as a reminder that life is short and that we *all* need to honor and take care of our minds and bodies. My mother was barely retired after working most of her life. She was only 68 years old. My belief at the time was that she did not have much and that she'd had a rough life filled with hardship and sadness. I later realized that her legacy was so much more than I ever gave her credit for. My mother was a strong Latina woman who could bounce back from anything. Whether she had money issues, poor health, failed relationships, or anything else, she always found a way to live her life joyfully no matter the circumstance.

Her greatest achievement was not only birthing, loving, and caring for her three sons, but having the will and strength to do whatever it took to raise her children as a single parent. I was the middle child and had a history of not getting along with my family; I was always labeled a troublemaker. After speaking with her doctor, the moment of truth came. Before stepping into my mom's hospital room, I found myself having second thoughts about seeing her. The last time we had spoken, she had told me that she never wanted to see me again. However, something visceral inside me told me to see her, make amends, and love her as long as I could. I knew her future was uncertain, but I did not know how she would react when she saw me. Committed to love, forgiveness, and creating a new relationship with family, I walked into the room with no regrets. Although she was surprised, her face lit up with joy. Tears and infectious smiles emerged from both of us, and I could see and feel the love she had for me regardless of our past issues. I experienced a powerful lesson in forgiveness as we loved, laughed, talked, and simply enjoyed our time together. We were completely present to the moment and no longer conscious of our circumstances, past or future.

My mother passed away 12 days after we had reconnected, on September 22, 2009. Although she had transitioned, her next great success came a few days after her passing, when many of her friends and family came together to honor and celebrate her life. The lesson that I realized from this experience was that success is in the eye of the beholder. With approximately 7 billion people on the planet, success could simply be feeding your family. In this case, my mother's life was a success as she was honored for her contributions as an amazing human being. It was clear from everyone I spoke to that she had loved, supported, and profoundly affected so many lives.

The passing of my mother was a difficult time for my estranged family and me. It would have been easier for me to go back to my life and just carry around the guilt and sadness.

However, in the weeks following, several family members and friends remained close and got together nightly to grieve, heal, pray, and remember her by sharing stories of her life. I believe we all found healing in our expressions of love for her.

When I'm healed, I'm not healed alone
—A Course in Miracles

We all have the ability to choose the way we move forward and the experience we have as the result of any circumstance.

In the circumstance of my mother passing away, the blessings and lessons were that a loving family was brought back together to remember her and reconnect with each other to create new loving relationships.

Today, I have an inveterate tendency to ask myself,

- *What are the lessons and the blessings for every challenging circumstance that I encounter?*

- *Are my circumstances really difficult, or did I make up that they were?*

- *What is this situation here to teach me?*

It is important for me to remember that facts are facts and that the only meaning of any situation is the one I attach to it.

I learned that I could choose to be responsible for my own experiences and learn and grow from them. Life will continue to happen. It is up to me to generate the life, love, and success that I want for my family and me.

After missing three weeks of work, I returned to what I experienced as an uncomfortable and different environment.

At the time I was a senior account manager for a Fortune 500 company with the responsibility to maintain and grow a base of over $15 million in company revenue. I acknowledged that my job performance had been affected by my lack of focus, and my performance numbers were down significantly. However, after 23 years of a successful track record, I truly believed I would quickly bounce back to create the results that I knew I was capable of achieving. After a few tough weeks of putting out fires, my immediate manager asked to meet with me and said that our vice president of sales would be joining us.

I remember the day clearly: It was raining outside, and as I arrived for our meeting in a cold, large conference room, I could sense that something was not right.

I did not know what to expect, but I believed I was prepared for anything. The vice president immediately took control of the meeting and without any hesitation told me that I was being pulled out of my job and replaced. He was aware of my recent time off and told me that he was sorry for my loss. However, he and my manager felt that I needed a change. He shared some performance results with me, and I quickly became defensive and emotional.

The most hurtful moment came when the vice president told me that this decision was made because I was not living up to my full potential. I had 90 days to improve my performance or I would be fired. After 23 years of loyalty and success, I felt my world collapsing all around me. This was my career and livelihood, how I fed my family, paid my bills, and put a roof over our head. I attempted to challenge the decision with specific results and activities before sadly surrendering.

The vice president walked out of the room to give me a few moments to calm down and talk to my manager, who was apologetic but made me aware that it could have been worse and that I needed to do well in my new position.

At the time, it was a huge blow to my ego, and I was extremely embarrassed. I felt that the company I had worked so hard for had given up on me, that I was being judged for numbers and not as the valuable asset I believed I was. "You are not living up to your full potential" echoed in my ears. Although the words were painful to hear, I later realized that it was the feedback I needed at that time.

After a few minutes talking to my manager, I began to experience a breakthrough and noticed a complete shift in my attitude. I immediately walked out of the conference room and apologized to the vice president for being defensive and rude. I then thanked him for the new opportunity and assured him that I would improve my performance.

This could have been a challenging time for me as it was only three weeks since my mother had passed away. However, I knew in my heart that this was another opportunity to bounce back successfully from yet another circumstance.

Being responsible for my experience I began to ask myself,

- *What were the lessons here? To stay focused, work hard, and never take anything for granted?*
- *What was the blessing here? Was it to be grateful that I still had a job in these tough economic times, or that I was given a second chance to prove myself?*

I was responsible for my circumstances, and my actions had led me to this moment. The feedback was a wake-up call to take inventory of where I was in my career and life, and to figure out how I would choose to grow and move forward. Life and careers will continue to happen. It is up to me to create the life, career, and success that I want to experience.

This is where the irony of this story begins. I call it the unintentional, intentional result of wanting to step into my true passion. For the past few years, I had been looking to change positions and even considered leaving my well-paying job so that I could do something that I truly felt inspired to do for the rest of my career. Although I had experienced success in sales, I really wanted to contribute to the success of others. The art of coaching, training, and mentoring others to be successful became my true passion after taking some personal development courses. Ironically, the position that I was being "demoted" to was a sales coaching and training position.

I began my new position coaching and training 14 sales representatives. Most of them were considered underperforming. However, I was committed to supporting them in living up to their full potential no matter our circumstances. To accomplish this, I began by sharing some lessons I had learned. One lesson was to distinguish our interpretation of mistakes and failures from the facts of any situation. It was not easy for everyone to learn how to manage their experiences and surrender to the facts of what actually happened. After several months of observing, coaching, and providing feedback, I celebrated with my team their outstanding achievements; several of them were promoted to account managers.

As a result of my coaching performance, I was taken off the 90-day notice within the first month of being in my new position. My ultimate satisfaction came from contributing to the success of others with no expectation of anything in return.

I was blessed to have this opportunity to be where I wanted to be and to do what I love. During this process, I was able to reinvent the perception my management team had of me. The vice president was very pleased with my results, and I was asked to take on a much bigger coaching role throughout our organization. Today, I can humbly and gratefully say that I am happy and passionate and love what I do. It's okay to earn a large salary too.

- *Is it possible that we are already successful and just don't realize it because of our points of view?*

- *Are you ready to step into your next level of growth and success? Remember your strengths, gifts, and how truly great you are.*

Just when you think your life is spiraling out of control, a renewed point of view may reveal that your life is actually spiraling in control.

Circumstances, situations, considerations, events, setbacks, and rough patches only mean what you say they mean. They will continue to show up at critical times of your life. See the facts for what they truly are. It is up to you to choose how you experience the events in your life and to learn the lessons and blessings they reveal. Remember to have the resiliency and perseverance to work through any situation without ever compromising your well-being and who you truly are. You are not your circumstances.

Life is full of limitless possibilities. The only limits that we have are the ones that we impose on ourselves. If success is in the eye of the beholder, it is up to us to envision and choose a successful and wonderful life.

Biography

Henry Maltez

HENRY MALTEZ is a sales performance coach with a passion to inspire and contribute to the success of others. He holds a master's degree in organizational management and a bachelor of arts in business management. Henry has 24 years of experience in management, sales, and consulting at a Fortune 500 company. He also uses his strong leadership and experience to make a difference for others as a mentor, public speaker, trainer, and success coach.

Contact Information

www.nextlevolution.com
henrymaltez@live.com
415-624-6000

Chapter 21

Everyone Has a Story, and This Is Mine

by Chico Humberto Ruiz Sanchez

We all have our own stories to tell. Mine isn't any better or any worse than yours. It's simply my experience, and ultimately, we have only our own experiences to live by—and to learn from.

We don't control the lives we're born into, our parents, or even some of the events in our lives, but one thing we do control—our thoughts. How we view our lives and think about our situations and dreams will shape our success. Yes, it really is that simple. But of course, it isn't always easy.

I was born into a hard-working family in Pasadena, California, the oldest of four boys. When I was two years old, we moved to Mexico, where at five years old I spent my days with another boy, riding horseback all over the mountains—it was an experience of freedom that would shape the man I am today.

Throughout our lives, we are all climbing a mountain. Sometimes, the clouds cover the top, and we lose sight of where we're going. But those are the times we have to keep the vision of the mountaintop clear in our own minds and just keep climbing. There are many stops along the way, storms that force us to take shelter in the mountain villages. Sometimes, we get stuck in these villages, thinking this is as far as we're going to get.

One of the biggest storms of my life occurred a few years after we returned to Pasadena: My youngest brother, at two and a half years old, was hit by a car and died. We all witnessed it. After losing a child, 85% of parents divorce, but my parents didn't. My dad married alcohol to deal with his pain.

My brother's death left me mad at the world, yet it also gave me courage. The year before, I had been getting beat up all the time at school. But now, I didn't take crap from anybody. At 10 years old, I stood up for myself and earned respect.

I would take this courage with me, but I would also take the anger. My dad continued to drink, and I continued to fight. By high school, I was drinking and skipping school. On one occasion, I was out drinking with some kids (including the now-infamous Rodney King), when I was expelled for being under the influence on school grounds.

This was one of many wake-up calls in my life. I knew I would only get into more trouble if I went with my friends to the continuation school. The same courage that made it all too easy to get into fights was also what saved me. I appealed to the principal to let me back into school. He rejected me, but I didn't give up. I got dressed up in a suit and went to see the superintendent. He gave me another chance.

And it wouldn't be the last time I got a second chance in life.

Later that year, after having some beers, friends and I climbed into a stock 1965 VW bug ragtop to go cruising Hollywood Boulevard. But on the way, heading southbound on the 110, the driver hit the middle embankment, the car started to fishtail, he hit it again, lost control, and the car began to flip. I was in the back seat, and I just remember suddenly being upside down, skidding. The back window popped out, and the roof scraped against the cement, sending giant sparks up all around us, and all I could think was that I did not want to die. We rolled over and over and eventually landed upright, with the engine throbbing at high idle. I thought the car was going to blow up, so I scrambled out of there.

It didn't blow up, and we all walked away with minor injuries. But later, when I went back to pull the engine out of the VW, I saw what a wreck it was. Completely demolished. We should have been dead.

God saved us that day. And the lesson was not wasted on me. When you're under the influence, you're not 100%. With so much in life out of our control, why give up any more than we have to?

The thing about getting knocked down in life is that the more you pick yourself up and keep going, keep climbing your mountain, the more confidence you build that the next time you're knocked down, you'll be able to get up again. And when you realize that this is true, you can start to see just how successful you can really be in this life simply by not ever giving up.

I was starting to have a real sense that there was more out there for me. I was still alive for a reason. Life was about more than just surviving. At 17, I finally tried out for my high school football team. I had always wanted to play football, had dreamed of playing Pop Warner, but my parents didn't understand the culture of it. And I had spent previous years just trying to survive my environment—stuck in a village with my friends, unable to find the path out. Now it was time to do more, to start climbing again toward my dreams. That took a new kind of courage. And it was rewarded.

I learned discipline from football, and I gained a new level of self-respect. The coach used me as an example of a player with heart. I didn't give up, even though I wanted to. Even though my parents never came to the games, not even when we played our rival school in the Rose Bowl. They didn't know why it was important to me. We only know what we know. By this point in my life, I had learned that you have to cheer yourself on. You can't wait on other people because you can't control what they do. You can only control yourself.

After the football season was over, I started thinking about a career. I had been working since I was 12, but now I was thinking about more than just a job. When I went to a fire explorer program at a Pasadena fire station, I knew what I wanted to do with my life.

But even with the courage, discipline, and self-respect I'd learned by this point in my short life, I still could not control everything. My dad still had a drinking problem, and I had prayed and prayed that he would stop. Then one night, I told God I was done praying. I had lost my faith.

The very next evening, my dad and my uncle were in the wrong place at the wrong time, and both were shot.

My uncle eventually died from his bullet wound. My dad survived with a bullet next to his spinal cord. The doctors said he should have been dead or at least paralyzed. It took him a year to recuperate, but he did recover, and he quit drinking and became a full-time dad.

My dad had been stuck for years, and it took a bullet to show him how to start climbing again.

I had to put my dream of becoming a firefighter on hold and get a full-time job to take care of my family. But I didn't forget my dream. I *knew* I would become a firefighter. As soon as things were stable back home, I continued pursuing that dream, but then life got in the way again, but this time, through events I did control. I got my girlfriend pregnant, and we got married far sooner than we had ever planned.

So I was back to working full time to take care of my new family. I pursued my dream on weeknights and some weekends. I could have given up. But the thing is, I already knew I was going to achieve my dream, so giving up just wasn't an option. The courage, discipline, self-respect, persistence, and sense of responsibility for my life that I had learned through my experiences were all there to support my vision of who I could be.

You are who you think you are. You become who you think you will be—who you *know* you will be.

When I tested for the Huntington Beach Fire Department, 2,700 applicants were invited to take the written test, and of that number, 800 passed to take the physical abilities test, and of that, they took only 300 to the first wave of oral interviews. From those interviews, only 45 made it to the chief's interview. They would hire 8.

After the first oral interviews, letters were sent out letting applicants know where they placed. I didn't receive a letter. But I did receive a phone call inviting me to the chief's interview. The morning of my interview, I found out from another candidate that only 45 had made it this far. I hadn't received a letter telling me where I'd placed, so I thought, wow, I just barely made it.

But I went into my interview confident anyway. I wanted this. I knew I would be a firefighter. After the interview I was told I would get a call on Saturday if I'd been chosen.

When I got home, my letter was waiting for me. I hadn't just barely made it. I was number one of the first set of interviews. I'd had good reason to be confident the whole time, but I didn't even know it!

They called on Friday to let me know I got the job, and when I went in to get fitted for uniforms and gear, they told me I was the only one called on Friday. They called me before everyone else because of my attitude.

Attitude is everything. Life is all about positive attitude. My glass is not half empty, but it's not half full either. It's completely full. I walked into that interview knowing I would be a firefighter. It didn't matter that I thought I'd barely made the interviews in the first place. In my mind, my glass was already full.

Having achieved that dream, I moved on to new dreams. I dreamed of setting us up so we would never want. Getting out of debt, buying a house, buying a bigger house when we outgrew that one with our four kids, and then yet a bigger one. I continued to learn on the job, expanding my skills and specialties, leading others to become the best they can be at everything they do. There is always more for me out there. More to learn, more to do, more to dream.

Once you reach a certain point in your life's climb, you'll naturally find yourself in a leadership position, guiding others up the mountain. My experiences in life, good and bad, have instilled some of the most important qualities a leader can have, including humility, compassion, and patience. I never forget what I've gone through and the mistakes I've made that have shaped who I am. This enables me to be respectful of others, patient with their different ways of climbing up their own mountain, and compassionate for what they are going through. We share the celebration of our successes and aren't too embarrassed to learn from our failures as a team and as individuals.

But even with these qualities, no one will follow you if they don't trust you. No matter who you are or who you lead, you have to have integrity and responsibility. When you do what is right whether anyone is watching you or not, and when you take responsibility for your own actions, people trust you and know they can depend on you. They also learn these qualities from your example, so that you can depend on them.

We all make mistakes. But leadership requires having the wisdom to learn from mistakes and not repeat them, and being resourceful enough to find answers even when you don't know them so that people can depend on you to lead them safely around fallen boulders in the path, ever onward toward the top. Leaders never stop learning any more than they stop dreaming.

Everyone has a different story to tell, but we're all climbing that mountain in life. And many of us are leading others to the top. If you think you've reached as high as you can go, *you have.* If you know you can climb higher, *you will.* Enjoy the view along the way, but don't forget, no matter what happens—keep climbing.

Biography

Chico Humberto Ruiz Sanchez

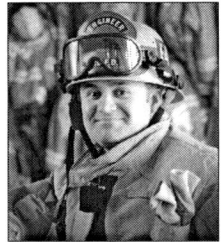

CHICO HUMBERTO RUIZ SANCHEZ is a 17-year firefighter/engineer HAZMAT specialist and honor guard member for the Huntington Beach Fire Department. Throughout his career, he has dedicated himself to continually learning and improving his leadership skills and knowledge because he believes "Your present is your future. What you do today becomes your tomorrow." Chico is currently pursuing a bachelor's degree in occupational safety and health from Columbia Southern University and playing bass drums for the Orange County Regional Firefighter Pipes and Drums. Married for 23 years, he and his wife, Jennifer, live in Temecula, California, with their four children, Christopher, Johnathan, Stephanie, and Michael.

Contact Information

www.chicohrsanchez.com

Chapter 22

How I Generate $260,957 in Sales in Five Days While I Sleep

by Thomas Hoi

After reading *Rich Dad, Poor Dad,* by Robert Kiyosaki, I was inspired to become an entrepreneur and take charge of my own financial freedom. Sticking to an 8-5 job is just not for me, and I'm hungry for success. I gave up the chance to study for my degree course in Singapore even though I was offered two places in the local universities.

Zero Sales Experiences

Without any sales background, I joined a network marketing company and started my entrepreneurial journey. I learned all the basics of selling, and off I went to talk to my friends and relatives about our company's products and opportunities.

Like what most network marketers experience, all my friends and relatives started to avoid me like the plague! Soon I had fewer friends to talk to and became miserable.

Once my "warm list" was exhausted, I went to cold calling and started to do road shows and exhibitions, where I would display my skin care products on a counter and promote them to shoppers, hoping they would not only buy but be so amazed by the results that they would in turn become my downline salespeople and start promoting the same products.

This way of selling my products worked initially, but soon I was standing at the booth the entire day for more than 12 hours without closing any sale. Not to mention I needed to pay for the daily rental. This lasted for more than a year, and I finally decided that this wasn't working. I was getting depressed with no income coming in.

Online Marketing to My Rescue

In April 2007, on the brink of quitting network marketing and going back to the reality of life, that is, getting a job, I stumbled upon the Internet and saw advertisements about becoming a millionaire by selling products online while sleeping!

Naturally, I thought all this was a scam, but I remembered reading in the news that real people were actually making money online, so I decided to give it one last try. I signed up for an Internet marketing course online and followed closely what they taught and put it into action. . . .

And I was totally amazed at the course content. What I learned about selling from the network marketing company was totally useless. It had worked 20 years ago, but in today's context, it simply doesn't. Online marketing is one of the most cost-effective way of getting prospects to call you and buy from you. No hard-selling tactics, customers get what they want, and both parties are happy.

The old school of selling is dead because nobody likes to get cold calls about something they aren't interested in. When you get a cold call from somebody you don't know, trying to sell you something you are not interested in, how do you feel? Disgusted? Frustrated? You might even feel annoyed for the rest of the day, and this can interrupt whatever you are doing and even affect your job performance.

Yet, this is the same way of prospecting for customers that is taught in all network marketing companies and even in most sales organizations!

To prove that online marketing works, I started to write some articles and posted them on top article directories like ezinearticles. com, and instantly, I became an expert author in my field.

Within six months, I got my first online sale—an e-book. My commission was only about $20. "Six months' effort for $20. Are you kidding me, Thomas?" you may be thinking.

Although this was little money, the sale proved that I could make money online. My breakthrough came toward the end of the year, when I made more than $1,000 in a single day using the exact methods that I had used to make my first sale online.

Now I'm completely convinced that this stuff works, and I use everything I learned and apply it to my network marketing business. Guess what? This works like a charm. I'm able to build websites where my prospect can find me after searching for what they want in Google. When they reach my website, they are required to submit their name and e-mail because they need to make an appointment with me so that I can check their skin condition. (I'm still selling skincare products.) Because of this, I was mistaken as a "skin doctor," even though I brand myself as the product consultant. I'm only selling the product and know little about dermatology.

So you can guess that by the time people came down for an appointment with me, they were already fully sold. They viewed me as an authority (like a real doctor talking to a patient) and accepted any recommendations I suggested. Using this technique, I was able to have more than a 90% closing rate!

Rejections? Price concerns? This does not happen to me at all! If you can master this strategy and apply it in your business, you could be increasing your sales by a 300% in a short time.

I have taught this same strategy to my downline salesperson, and she too is having excellent results— no more rejections, and she is also seen as an authority figure in her customers' eyes. The major advantage in leveraging on online marketing is that you only spend time with *qualified prospects* who will likely give you the sale, filtering out those who could be wasting your precious time.

Local Business Online Marketing

Recently, I discovered many local business websites are not optimized for local users. Take, for example, when people want Lasik surgery: They will probably type "Lasik Cleveland" or "Lasik Surgery Cleveland" into Google because they want to find a Lasik surgeon near their home.

Sensing some opportunity here, I decide to create a new local website targeting the Lasik surgery niche in my country. I did some research and found that people are searching for the keyword phrase "Lasik Singapore" in Google. I then set up a website for that niche, and within six months, I was ranked in the top three for that highly competitive keyword phrase.

Many Lasik surgeons are advertising through Google Adwords for the same keyword phrase for more than $5 a click, while I'm getting it for free! Plus, my prospects see me as an authority in this industry since my website is ranked so high in Google, which gives me the edge over my competitors. (Note: I'm not a Lasik surgeon, so I partner with an eye doctor in Singapore.)

From this experiment, I realized that it's easy to rank for local businesses. I ventured into my next project and *generated $260,957 in sales in just five days while I sleep.*

The new website took only about three months to get to the number one position in Google for a highly searched two-keyword phrase. There were days when I got thousands of unique visitors a day, peaking at more than 6,000. Today, this website has over 900 opt-ins, which means I now have a database of hot leads to whom I can sell new products over and over again forever. This is why millionaire online marketers say, "The money is in the list."

All this happens because I'm able to predict a trend. I know *exactly what keyword phrase my prospects will type* into Google to search for what they want. With previous success from online marketing, I managed to grab this opportunity and sell my products to a group of "hungry crowds," who came to my site with their credit cards in hand.

No rejections, no price concerns—they just buy online! And yes, all the sales transactions were done on autopilot, without me talking to a single customer.

In summary, these are the three basic steps you can use:

1. Find a hungry crowd (people who are desperate and ready to buy *now*!)

2. Find out what they really want (their hot buttons, the end results they want to see)

3. Give it to them (optimize your website for the targeted keyword phrases)

Instant Traffic Boost

Want some instant visitors to your website? These ninja tactics will bring you tons of leads and sales if you use them the right way. But before doing this, I highly recommend you develop an *opt-in list* so you can capture your website visitors' names and e-mail addresses by offering a gift, such as a free e-book. (If you are not sure how this is done, go to my website at www.ThomasHoi.com for an example.)

Are you ready? Good!

Ninja Tactic #1—Press Release

Create your own press release. Imagine your company, products, or services being featured in the news. What sort of credibility will you get? Without a doubt, people will see you as the authority and will gladly buy from you, eliminating your competitors.

The easiest and most effective way is to submit your press release to PRWeb.com. Your press release should be newsworthy and written from the perspective of a "journalist." The basic option costs $80, and once accepted, your press release will be distributed to major news websites like Yahoo! News, Google News, Topix, journalists, and bloggers so that your products or services can be found everywhere on the web. This could potentially increase your search engine position and drive more customers to your website.

Ninja Tactic #2—Gain Instant Market Share

You have seen big corporations buy up small companies to instantly increase market share. You may be surprised, but such scenarios are also happening in the online world. You can literally go to flippa.com and scoop up tiny websites that already have targeted traffic and top ranking in the search engines.

Such websites can be bought starting at several hundred dollars. Those that have a history of consistent income for at least 12 months will cost anything from four to six figures, depending on the monthly income.

If you are good enough, you will be able to spot some gems, buy them for several hundred dollars, and then generate leads you can send to your own website to get sales. You can request traffic and income proof from these website owners to make sure the site fits your target market.

Ninja Tactic #3—Natural Type-in Traffic

Sex.com was sold in 2010 for a record $13 million to Clover Holdings Limited. Fund.com was sold for $9.9 million, and Diamond.com was sold for $7.5 million. All are just domain names and do not include any website development.

Why are these domain names sold for such high prices? They are names that people like you and me will just type into the browser conveniently without going through any search engines. Such domain names are brandable and easy for people to remember, so they command high value.

In recent years, more and more companies are buying such domain names to generate leads. Because this is highly targeted traffic, the conversion rate (visitors becoming customers) is much higher than the rate from search engines. You can visit Sedo.com and buy up premium domain names related to your products or services to get an edge over your competition.

No matter who you are or how much sales experience you have, you can make a ton of money online. Follow these simple techniques and you too can wake up to hundreds of thousands of dollars.

Biography

Thomas Hoi

THOMAS HOI began his entrepreneurial journey as a network marketer in 2005 with no sales experience. Like many network marketers, he discovered that the traditional way of selling is dead, and he stumbled upon online marketing, where he learned to generate leads online to get people to come to him to buy. Using online strategies, Thomas generated $260,957 in sales in just five days without ever talking to any customers.

Contact Information

www.ThomasHoi.com
info@thomashoi.com
www.facebook.com/thomas.hoi
twitter.com/thomashoi
http://www.youtube.com/thomashoi
+65-9-768-0834

Chapter 23

Your Partner in Crime
THE SUBCONSCIOUS MIND

by Oliver T. Asaah

What is the subconscious mind?

How is the subconscious programmed?

How can we access programs in the subconscious?

How can we reprogram the subconscious?

These are the questions I address in this chapter.

What Is the Subconscious Mind?

The subconscious is the guardian angel of the conscious mind and the queen motivator of our actions.

The subconscious influences every second of our lives in everything we do or fail to do; it is dictated by programs that have been systematically installed in our subconscious starting from birth. It is our partner in crime that micromanages the roles we play as actors, participants, and spectators in the theatre of life.

Some of these thoughts are empowering, others disempowering. Disempowering ideas are those that hold us back from exploring, exploiting, and manifesting our passion and unleashing our full potential. Empowering ones help us get closer to our destiny. Unfortunately, many minds focus on disempowering thoughts, which often over-power the positive programs in our subconscious.

How Is the Subconscious Programmed?

The subconscious is the invisible master pilot of our actions. It tele-guides our thinking; our thinking dictates our actions; and our actions show who we are.

In the Nweh and in some other cultures in the Cameroons, twins are believed to possess some magical powers: they can bring good and bad luck to their family. Twins can inadvertently hurt family members by mysteriously inflicting severe pain. Upon satisfying their demand, they just as mysteriously fix their fetish deeds.

Once upon a time, at the age of about six, one of my step twin sisters was upset with me, and she promised to sprain my leg. She kept staring at my right leg; consequently, after a while, when I stood up, I realized I couldn't walk. My right leg was hurting me, and I coaxed her to forgive me and return my leg to normal. Instantaneously, my leg felt fine.

This belief like many others has existed from time immemorial; it is held to be true and inextricably interwoven with the lifestyle of believers. Some beliefs might not be true, but extreme belief and faith makes them seem real to us. The subconscious is programmed in a similar way.

Three dimensions encode the subconscious at varying degrees: *persons* (family, teachers, mentors, peers, friends, associates), *place* (environment), and *things* (experiences, media, books, films). They determine by whom, how, where, when, and why we acquire our programs. Asking and answering these questions will facilitate the process of reprogramming our subconscious.

Subconscious programming starts from conception: According to Joseph Susedik, "Talking to children in the womb has a tremendous impact on their development." He recommends a calm, serene environment for a pregnant mother. A solemn atmosphere ensures the birth of a child with utter trust in the parent. A Dallas *Times Herald* article on May 15, 1982, described Joseph and Jitsuko Susedik's belief that any parent can raise brilliant children; they just need phonics, environment, and curiosity—the earlier the better. "Only if the child has complete trust can he or she be taught. You must teach your children with love, gentleness and only at a time they are willing to learn," Susedik says.

According to Zig Ziglar, in his *Raising Positive Kids in a Negative World,* Dr. Carole Taylor, head of the Tolatr Academy in Pittsburgh, believes that once children master phonics, they can read anything, even college texts. Dr. Taylor's daughters at 10 and 14 years of age were enrolled part time in pre-med courses in a community college. This is a good example of how the person, place, and thing factors are responsible for programming the subconscious for peak performance.

How Can We Access Programs in the Subconscious?

This is a journey into the realm of our being to enjoy the human endowments—self-awareness, imagination, conscience, and independent will—that differentiate us from animals.

Just DEEP it (Dig, Employ, Expect, Profit) and the salt and the sweat will yield the malt. Unlike consulting a doctor when we are sick for diagnostics and prescription, we have to DOCTOR ourselves in reprogramming the subconscious; that is my experience. To me,

DOCTOR means **D**iagnose, **O**perate, **C**ure, **T**reat, **O**xygenate, and **R**espect. The exercise is very personal, serene, and engaging.

Faith is a state of mind which can be induced through repeated affirmations or instructions to the SUBCONSCIOUS MIND through the principle of autosuggestion.
—Napoleon Hill

I started with an insight and ended up with sight; I have seen tangible results in my life, such as an impeccable positive mindset, which is the reason I am writing this chapter. My baseline of positive attitude is fantastic, then super fantastic, and finally super duper fantastic. My contagious positive attitude has given me beatitude at my jobsite, earning me the nickname Mr. Fantastic! I have seen colleagues who were less enthusiastic and other employees who were generally moody brighten up and raise their level of happiness when we met and communicated. This is the mirror neuron effect as described in positive psychology: Our attitude, whether it is positive or negative, tends to contaminate the people around us by lighting up their neurons in response to the attitude exhibited to them.

Begin with the outcome in mind. You have to see the project from start to finish by visualizing how the successful result will affect your life. Believe in the magic of believing prior to the process and see it manifest itself. Take a leap of faith forward into the unknown and see your undertaking fructify. If you believe it, it will work for you, and vice versa. Physicians have testified that patients who belief in their prescriptions see the best results.

1. Grab paper and a pen and look for a serene place. For instance, take your notepad, pen, and a flashlight into a closet.

2. Prepare your mind for utter concentration and laser focus.

3. Start examining your past, present, and future life, especially your beliefs, goals, and dreams.

4. Jot down all thoughts that come to mind: empowering and disempowering.

5. Exhaust all thoughts until they begin to repeat themselves.

6. Separate programs into group (A), empowering, and group (B), disempowering.

7. Transcribe your groups into two lists of keywords with the positive heading (A): for example, rich, happy, healthy, lucky, generous, successful, likeable, intelligent, confident, strong, proactive, good-humored, smiley, blessed, hard-working, attractive..., and the negative heading (B): for example, poor, unhappy, sickly, bewitched, dishonest, stupid, weak, unlucky, quarrelsome, hated, moody, greedy, unattractive, procrastinating, lazy, self-doubting....

Group B will dumbfound and daze you, but like harnessing a crystal ball, this exercise will take you to the crest of your future. It demands tremendous personal effort. When the daze is overwhelming, take a break, but do not freak; resume after regaining sanity.

Negative programs also come from errors we committed in the past, unrealized dreams and aspirations, unforgiving and retributive attitudes learned from unforgiving and vengeful people around us, from hating self and others, and even from liking and loving self and others. The entire process is an ORDEAL: Open, Right, Developmental, Enforcement, and Action for Life. It is the right action. Just be open and enforce it for your personal development. Eventually, your energy will lead to unstoppable synergy!

You are the way you are because that's the way
you want to be. If you really wanted to be any different,
you would be in the process of changing.
—Fred Smith

We are 100% in control of the process of decoding and re-encoding our subconscious and unleashing our potential just as we are in control of our attitude. The difference is that our negative programs might be influencing our attitude. Let's program our subconscious to work for us.

The greatest discovery of my generation is that a human being
can alter his life by altering his attitude.
—William James

How Can We Reprogram the Subconscious?

To be blind is bad, but worse is to have eyes and not see.
—Helen Keller

Synchronize the final process; fill the vacuum left by decoded negative programs with positive ones. It is the most difficult but groovy part of the process. Our burning desire to succeed will hone our power to alter the status quo, release our potential, and unshackle us. Unlike our minds, the subconscious never goes to sleep over our lifetime.

I came up with this formula to clear my path: Steadfast, Proactive, Assertive, Discipline, and Emphatic (SPADE). I decided to pick up my SPADE and dig my goldmine. This metaphor propelled me to unclutter my mind and get rid of the noise that held me back from moving forward. I apply SPADE in my daily activities.

SPADE forms the north arc, and *action* forms the south arc, meeting in the middle to form the circle of life. The diameter of this circle tells us: *Do it now; there is no tomorrow!*

Decoding and Reprogramming Process

1. Determine the original cause of negative programs.

2. Ask what fuels your programs.

3. Figure out the negative programs' support systems (person, place, or thing?)

4. Figure out the supportive energy for positive programs (person, place, or thing?)

5. Use the answers you discover to handle corresponding situations promptly and assuredly.

6. Note positive programs against negative ones. For example: rich versus poor.

7. Replace disempowering programs with corresponding empowering ones.

8. Declare, affirm, meditate.

9. Celebrate success and progress.

10. Repeat process until corresponding positive programs replace negative ones.

I use the mirror technique created by Dr. Laura De Giorgio in the decoding and encoding procedure. I look at myself squarely in the eyes, building trust and bonding with myself first. Look in the mirror and ask yourself: Am I poised for change? Be honest. The mirror reflects our image back to us, facilitates introspection, reaching into the subconscious to install our new software for our probing inquisitorial response and positive drive.

The mirror technique helps translate our daily mantras, pep ourselves up, and prime our "limitless possibilities" pump. We have to be, do, and then have, in that order. Never try to have, be, and then do. Are you taking full advantage of your positive programs? Release their full potential. In the ORDEAL we shall face obstacles, objections, mesmerisms, dilemmas . . . but our faith will resuscitate us.

I experienced a rollercoaster in some programs and momentary crestfalls in others. SPADE, daily meditations, declarations, and affirmations helped me get over most of them. Listen to and watch motivational and inspirational recordings. Adjust or quit the relational illness environment and develop a nourishing mindset. READ (Rise Every day Above Death) and STUDY (Seek Tune Up Drive Yourself) consistently. Reading is the first step. Studying what you just read tunes you up so you can apply yourself correctly through acquired knowledge—that is power!

Be relentless in mastering your new positive programs with practice and exercise. The more engraved disempowering software was in your subconscious, the harder you have to work to reprogram it. I revisited the reprogramming process several times, and I still do for the hard ones. I believe the earlier in life one uses this technique, the more reversible the situation is. Meticulously unlearn the negative programs and learn positive ones. Once positive ones take root, practice and accentuate their benefits to prevent negative programs from resurfacing. The procedure is simple but not easy. Everyone can learn the art, apply the tact, earn the act, tell the fact, and sell their story.

My first name is OLIVER (Open Life Invitation and Values Earn Riches). I am inviting you to open up your life by giving reprogramming a chance because I am living proof that it works; this is not pontification. While in the process, I realized that I needed help, an accountability partner. Incidentally my last name is ASAAH (Asking Seasoned Assistance Always Helps). That's how I decided to make my names acronyms to empower me in all my ventures. We always need help from a loved supportive one who can hold us accountable and measure our progress, who will commend or reprimand us accordingly. It must be someone we trust and respect enough to bestow our life's purpose on.

> *Were it not for Tanzing the native guide, Edmund Hilary would not have made the historic climb of Mt. Everest.*
> —John Maxwell

Do not frustrate yourself by expecting exquisite performance initially. Donald Trump's *Apprentice* became the number one reality show on NBC after several failures, but he followed his instincts against expert advice; hone your partner in crime for invincible results.

Everyone has empowering and disempowering programs. Just make sure the ratio greatly favors positive ones. Ninety-seven percent of the population works for 3% because our programming influences our choices. We can alter that equation by reprogramming our subconscious mind.

Biography

Oliver T. Asaah

One of 24 children, and having a bachelor's in law, OLIVER ASAAH's experience is a powerful mélange of human relations and conflict resolution. He has several years of experience in network marketing in multiple companies and is currently a wellness entrepreneur, building one of the biggest organizations in Genewize, DNA-customized health, wellness, and skincare solutions company. He is a speaker and mentor/coach with a passion for motivating and inspiring people. Oliver has vested and harnessed the power of the subconscious through reprogramming and using his SPADE formula to maximize intuitive energy and synergy for personal and organizational achievement.

Contact Information

www.wealthpoolindustries.com

oliverasaah@yahoo.com

301-537-2068

Chapter 24

The Ingredients for Achieving Success

by Dr. Steven Balestracci and Dr. Terresa Balestracci

Success is like a recipe; there are many ingredients. So, if there were a recipe for success, what would it be? Well, the first step is to have a dream, a reason, a why. Not having this is like taking a vacation without knowing where you are going. Next, you need to have a plan or a vision. These are the procedures to get to your destination, your roadmap, so to speak. After that you need the desire and passion to get you to your destination, your "fuel" to get you from point A to point B. This is vital to driving you toward your goal. Then, you need a support team or an accountability partner. This is very important so that you have people to encourage you along the way, helping you overcome the challenges you will undoubtedly face.

You may not always control the roadblocks along your journey, but two things you can control are your thoughts and with whom you surround yourself. Achieving success is not easy, but surrounding yourself with people who believe in you, who support and encourage you, will definitely accelerate the speed at which you can reach your dreams. This includes reading books that inspire you to succeed and grow as a person.

The last step in your recipe for success is to celebrate! When you achieve your goals and dreams and after every win along the way, you should rejoice and be thankful for the many blessings you have.

We believe that a key ingredient to achieving success at any level is having faith, not only in ourselves but most of all in God. We believe that God puts dreams in our minds and hope in our hearts for a reason. He truly wants us to have the many blessings that He has to offer. We are truly thankful for the dreams and desires that the Lord has placed in our hearts and minds and the daily courage He graces us with to live them out.

Our favorite quote on success is by George Sheehan: "Success means having the courage, the determination, and the will to become the person you believe you were meant to be." We love this quote because it is also the true meaning of success. Nowhere in the quote does it talk about how much money you make or how many material objects you possess. This quote can truly be applied to any person and any situation. Without courage, you allow fear to prevent you from taking the next step that is vital in achieving success. Without determination, you allow challenges to prevent you from continuing on your path to being successful.

One of the major challenges that we believe holds people back from success is that of fear. Overcoming fear is one the most difficult things to do, but if a person does not overcome a fear that is a roadblock to achieving their goals, they will never achieve success associated with that goal or dream. We believe that any super-successful person has had to overcome many fears and obstacles along the way. Even though some of the steps you need to take on your journey may make you uncomfortable at times, understand that being uncomfortable is an indication that you are on the right path, and by pushing though, you will grow as a person and be another step closer to your dreams.

Think of small children who are learning to walk. First, they need courage to take the first step. Even after they try and fall down many times, they must keep going or they will never succeed in walking. If they were to allow their fear of falling to get in the way, they would never even try again. This is why we believe that it is an innate instinct for us to want to achieve. It is up to us whether we allow the challenges we face on our journey of success to strengthen us or to weaken us. We must simply decide to turn our challenges into strengths.

To us, success is pursuing your dreams and goals despite any and all the obstacles that may occur during the process. We have had many challenges in our businesses and in our personal lives, and we continue to today. Whether it is a two-month delay in the build-out of our office space, an employee who has stolen from us, one of our kids getting sick, or losing a loved one, we have faced these challenges and never lost sight of our dreams and goals. What we have realized as we have grown over the years through our experiences and education is that the challenges never stop coming, but how we react to them has changed. For example, a situation that five years ago would have distracted us and got us off the path to our goals for weeks or months now only lasts for hours or days.

A mindset that we have learned to draw upon is that of improvise, adapt, and overcome. This has allowed us to open our minds to how powerful they are. Many have spoken and written of the power of the mind: "Whatever the mind can conceive, it can achieve!" and as Henry Ford has said, "Whether you think you can . . . or you think you can't . . . you're right." Yoda said it all in the *Star Wars* series: "There is no try, there is only do or not do." An important concept that we teach our kids also speaks to the power of the mind: "Never let anyone's opinion of you become your reality unless it is a positive opinion!"

The greatest tip we have learned in life and business is forgiveness, being able to leave the past in the past. Not only is it vital to forgive others when they have wronged you, but it is just as important to forgive yourself. Not forgiving yourself can destroy your self-worth and send you down a path of self-destruction and mediocrity. Many times in our lives we have been presented with challenges, things that hurt us financially and emotionally, and we dwelled on them and allowed them to steal happiness from our lives and enthusiasm from our spirits. We have personally seen people carry baggage from the past and allow it to destroy their lives. They wind up getting ill, mentally and physically, and stand in the way of any chance at happiness and success they ever had. The personal growth and development training that we have experienced, especially in the last three years with our newest business venture, has made us reflect on those challenges from the past and realize how much they held us back and delayed and distracted us from our goals and dreams in the pursuit of our success.

Some of the most important keys in achieving success are having desire and passion. We both grew up in Italian American households, where there was a great deal of influence from many family members. Food was always present no matter what the occasion or lack of occasion. The main thing about this combination of family, food, and conversation was *passion* and *desire*. These people were very passionate and expressive, to say the least, about what seemed like everything they spoke of—a sporting event, last night's dinner, or a day at work. For most of them, their desire was to be more successful than the last generation, as was the last's generation's desire for them. It was evident that they were passionate about this desire and that this desire made them passionate. This love of life and people was a driving force in their pursuit of happiness and success and has influenced us and helped to define who we are today.

Other major influences are the role models and mentors that we have chosen to learn from. While we have many favorite authors, speakers, and educators, a few stand out. Two of our favorite role models are B. J. Palmer, developer of chiropractic and world-renowned educator and entrepreneur, and Warren Buffet, world-renowned entrepreneur and business mogul, because they represent success that was achieved through passion, desire, and vision. Two of our favorite mentors are Marc Accetta, world-renowned trainer, speaker, and entrepreneur, and Matt Morris, world-renowned best-selling author, speaker, and entrepreneur. Marc and Matt are both incredibly successful people who have taught us so much about life and helped us achieve our current level of success through their guidance, incredible leadership, and training. They both possess qualities that have taught us a great deal about leadership. They are passionate about teaching people to achieve the success that they have, which is a quality that we greatly admire.

The thing that we are most passionate about is helping people. This is why we pursued our careers in chiropractic. We feel that chiropractic has the ability to positively affect people's lives profoundly since we, as doctors and teachers, empower people to take a more active role in their health and well-being rather than being victims and passively existing through the symptom-based system that the current healthcare model offers. We also have passion and desire to help people through our other business in the industry of network marketing and travel. With this business we have learned personal growth and development skills, as well as the skills to create additional streams of income and to be able to assist others to achieve the same. As we experience wins in our businesses through helping people, we achieve spiritual and emotional wins for ourselves. This is the satisfaction that continues to motivate us to keep going in our pursuit of success.

Another desire we have as we continue to pursue our dreams is to make our children proud of us. We believe that the best way we can do this is to live with passion, have the courage to finish what we start, and lead by example. We try to be as mindful of this as possible as we raise our three children. We want them to have their own dreams that they desire to pursue, and we do not want to live vicariously through them and prevent them from reaching their full potential. In addition, we remind them that even when they have a class or subject that they really do not have much interest in, they should put forth effort, because they might just be surprised at the outcome, especially with regard to the growth of self-confidence and self-worth. When we were growing up, we always had the desire for our parents to be proud of us; however, now that we have kids, they are the ones we most want to make proud. We feel that achieving this would be one of the greatest successes in our lives.

As parents and successful business owners, we believe that you have to lead by example. Whether you see yourself as a leader or not, many of us are viewed that way because of the actions that we take and the way that we inspire the people around us. Leadership is really a combination of many qualities that an individual must possess. It is an action, not a position. A true leader is someone who can motivate people to take action through communication and representation as well as someone with the ability to overcome resistance to challenges to attain a common goal for the betterment of both the individual and the team. A great leader, Zig Ziglar, once said, "If you help enough other people get what they want, you get what you want."

Finally, for us, we have realized that success is a culmination of many attributes, with some of the main ones being faith, vision, passion, desire, belief, courage, resilience, attitude, confidence, forgiveness, humbleness, integrity, honor, purpose, patience, leadership, knowledge, and the application of knowledge.

We are truly blessed and humbled to have the opportunity to share some of our thoughts on success in order to positively affect the lives of others with the hopes that this will assist them on their journey of success.

Biography

Dr. Steven and Dr. Terresa Balestracci

STEVEN AND TERRESA met in Davenport, Iowa, while attending Palmer College of Chiropractic, where they both graduated with their doctor of chiropractic degrees. They have owned a successful chiropractic office in Bridgewater, New Jersey, for the past 15 years. They have also been involved in network marketing for the past 3 years with WorldVentures, where they are in the top 1% of the company's independent representatives. Steven and Terresa have three children, Michael, 14, Gianna, 10, and Cristian, 4, for whom they strive to achieve higher levels of success and for whom they desire to leave a legacy.

Contact Information

www.OurLifePassions.com
info@OurLifePassions.com
484-375-5380 / 484-375-5385

Chapter 25

Children Become Our Legacy

WHAT LEGACY WILL YOU LEAVE BEHIND?

by Jill Nieman Picerno

W hen people think of the legacy they want to leave behind, they usually think financially. However, when I was a child I knew that my legacy would be my children. I thought that the most important thing I could do for the world was raise my children into amazing adults. I always wanted to have two girls, sisters, because I never had a sister and always thought that would be so great. My wish came true. I was blessed with two incredible girls. My first daughter, Jacquelyn was born when I was 28 years old. Then two years and ten months later, Caitlyn was born.

I was fortunate enough to become a stay-at-home mom the day Jacquelyn was born, but this didn't just happen. My husband, at the time, and I worked hard to pay off debts and make sure that his income would provide for our family to live comfortably once I stayed home. As a CPA, I started my own practice for a while after Jacquelyn was born, running it from our home. I actually chose this career while in college specifically with this in mind. Parenting, not my CPA practice, would always be my number one job.

I have read so many books about children and child raising, talked about my children and their various stages of development with my friends and family, and even asked strangers their opinions about parenting. Once I began the parenting role, I set off toward creating my legacy. I knew that having an honest and completely open relationship with my girls when they were teenagers would be crucial to creating the legacy I wanted to leave behind.

Parenting is a tough job! It requires a ton of energy, and you need to realize that how you parent shapes your child's future. We all want the best for our children, but sometimes that gets lost in the day-to-day activities. We need to write down our goals for parenting. Look at how you were parented. What did you like about your parents' parenting styles and what didn't you like? Many of us rarely take the time to actually sit down and think this through.

Sit down right now and take out a sheet of paper. Let your mind go back in time and remember how your parents raised you. Write down everything that comes to your mind, without stopping, letting your thoughts flow. Keep writing until you believe you have captured their parenting styles on paper. Now the fun begins. We are all creatures of habit, so many of us just parent as we were parented. That doesn't need to be the case. What type of parenting style do you want your children to experience? How do you want your children to feel about you and them? Remember to start creating your legacy with the end in mind.

Parents often ask me how I created such an honest and completely open relationship with my girls. Many things help create our incredible relationships along the way, but I have had one rule from the beginning of my parenting role. This rule, I believe, was the foundation to my strong relationships with my children: No lying.

Lying is always wrong. My girls learned at a very early age to tell the truth. This was not an easy task to accomplish. Children will lie to their parents, especially to avoid being punished for something they did wrong in their parents' eyes. Like all children, my girls did not like to be punished, and they did lie to me to avoid it. They soon figured out, though, that when they lied to me to avoid being punished, their punishment became 10 times worse than if they had just told me the truth from the beginning. They also learned that if they told me the truth right away about what they had done wrong, they wouldn't get in as much trouble as if I had caught them in the act. This was a little bit of a reward for telling the truth right away. Both my girls learned this rule and realized that telling the truth had its benefits.

Parents should try to catch their children lying at an early age and instill in them the value of honesty. Become a great detective. Learn the body signals that occur when someone is lying to you. Children will usually delay answering your initial questions. When they finally do answer, their voices will have a slightly higher pitch to them. They may cover their mouth with their hands or rub their nose often. Facial expressions will change. Their face may look paler and stiffer, their nostrils may flare, and their lips may look thinner and tighter. Avoiding direct eye contact, squinting, or closing their eyes may also give them away. Their body may become stiffer, shoulders may be pulled up, and their elbows may be held close to their body. These are just a few of the body signals that parents may want to be on the lookout for.

Once you know your children are lying, take action. Do not explain to them how you know. All they need to know is that you know they lied. Then tell them this is unacceptable. Explain to them the initial punishment they would have received for the inappropriate behavior they lied about. Then let them know that since they lied to you about what happened, the punishment will be 10 times the initial punishment they would have received. Remember to have the punishment fit the inappropriate behavior, but make sure it is something you can and will follow through with. Your children need to realize that you were upset about their inappropriate behavior, but that you are so much more disappointed in the fact that they felt the need to lie to you. Children lie to avoid punishment, but they do not want to disappoint you, and lying creates disappointment.

When children start to reach the teenage years, this lying rule needs to be set in stone. You still need to be able to detect your child's body signals when he or she is lying. Realize also that this age is a very difficult stage in your child's development. Try to remember how you felt or acted as a teenager. Yes, that does scare some of us, and we don't want our children to make some of the same mistakes we did. However, they don't always learn from being told what to do and what not to do. They do need to make some of their own mistakes. Also, being overly strict does not seem to produce the best results in teens either. I know things about my girls' friends that their parents would not believe if I told them.

Parent without blinders on. The information I know about their friends becomes handy when trying to steer them toward a better path in life. Teenagers are influenced by their friends more than their parents. You just have to be one of their friends too, but always be the parent first and their friend second. Teenagers will not tell you that they like you being their parent and setting rules, but this honestly does make them feel loved. They know you care what happens to them. My girls think some of my rules are a little over the top, but they understand my reasoning behind them. They know they are loved. It's a fine line between having too many rules or too few rules or too strict rules or not strict enough rules. Building that honest and completely open relationship with your children will help guide you in setting your own rules for your teenagers.

This brings me to a question that has come up between my girls. Should I treat them differently? Yes and no. Yes, some rules should be the same, but every teenager is different. I remember having dinner with my girls one night, and Caitlyn began talking about one of her friends drinking her parents' alcohol. I asked Caitlyn, "Which friend is that?" Caitlyn proceeded to tell me, in so many words, that it was none of my business and that she didn't want me to tell the girl's parents. I then explained to her that she did not need to tell me which friend of hers was doing this, but then she would suffer the consequences of my parenting rules being different for her than for her sister. Of course, life is not fair. I continued explaining to Caitlyn that Jacquelyn has told me many things about her friends that I haven't mentioned to her friends' parents. My trust with Jacquelyn would be higher, and she would have more privileges related to hanging out with her friends than Caitlyn would.

Needless to say, Caitlyn decided to tell me which friend of hers was drinking her parents' alcohol, and we moved on from there. This information allowed me to steer her on a different life path without letting her know what I was actually doing. Instead of disallowing her to spend time with this girlfriend, which most likely would have steered her directly toward her, I began steering her more toward a different set of friends. This is just one example of the rewards of creating honest and completely open relationships with your children.

I have always kept my girls' secrets about their friends safe with me, except for one time. The only time I believe that I should tell another parent something about their teenager that my girls have shared with me in confidence is if it can be life threatening. I actually got my daughter's permission to talk to the teenager's parents, because she was worried about her friend's life as well. Everything, fortunately, turned out great.

The teenage years are always interesting. I love that my girls feel so comfortable coming to me with any questions they have, but when the teenage years rolled around, their questions became life-path altering. They asked about sex, drugs, boys, girls, and so many other important life topics. Sometimes when one of my girls would ask me a question, inside I was freaking out, but on the outside I acted like they had asked me, "What are we doing for dinner?" I was so proud of my girls being able to ask me any question they wanted. They knew that I didn't know everything, but I told them we could always find out the answer together.

One question I remember one of my girls asking me was "Do you die if you have sex before you're 19 years old?" My daughter was just entering her teenage years, and one of her friend's moms had told her friend that. So began the talk about sex. Of course I told her the truth, that you do not die if you have sex before you are 19 years old. I think that mother was trying to protect her daughter but didn't have an open relationship to talk things out. This then led us into a conversation about AIDS, STDs, and so on. Their questions were always a time to have discussions and for me to steer them in the direction I felt was best for them. I realized that no one can really control another person. So I have tried to give my girls as much information as I thought necessary for them to make the correct choices in life. They and I are glad we have this honest and completely open relationship. It hasn't always been easy, but it's always been worth it.

My life path continues today, creating my legacy—my incredible girls! This is how I measure success.

Biography

Jill Nieman Picerno

JILL NIEMAN PICERNO is a very proud mother and entrepreneur. She is a student of parenting, finance, real estate, and network marketing. She has a thirst for knowledge and loves to meet new people and visit new places around the world. Jill is a certified public accountant, owns several real estate properties, and has her own travel business. She is also in the process of creating her own parenting book.

Contact Information

www.travelgirls.biz
Jill@travelgirls.biz
303-400-5100

Chapter 26

How to Work Less, Earn More, and Live Free as a Lifestyle Entrepreneur

by Francis Ablola

If you spotted me at Starbucks grabbing my morning double espresso or white mocha, you wouldn't think much.

My normal work attire consists of a T-shirt, basketball shorts, and a pair of old flip-flops. Chances are I haven't shaved in a week, and my backwards cap is hiding the fact that I desperately need a haircut.

You'd probably never guess that I just wrapped up a marketing campaign for one of my clients that brought an additional seven figures in revenue, or that I'm masterminding a project that will bring in thousands of new potential customers in just a few weeks.

I operate under the radar, and that's the way I like it.

I call it being a . . .

Lifestyle Entrepreneur

I work only when I feel like it, with the people I like investing my time with, by my own rules from my Floridian beachfront office overlooking the Atlantic Ocean. The rest of the time you'll find me at home with my beautiful wife and my bouncing baby girl, traveling the country, meeting with fellow lifestyle entrepreneurs, and learning new skills that create massive results for me and my clients.

I love what I do, and it's exactly how I've designed it.

I don't say to this to brag or boast. I wasn't born with any special talents or advantages. I tell you this to say it's possible for you to design a business that supports *you* and your desired lifestyle.

I'd like to share with you how I went from being a 20-something college dropout, to corporate burnout, to living a life of *awesomeness* by design . . . and how you can do it too.

Why I Never Want to Grow Up!

It's easy to get lost in what the universe throws you. Long hours, stressful days, increasing frustration, lost time with family and friends—when you're not in control of your world, you accept this as status quo. So many people get caught up in the day-to-day, working for a living and forgetting to create a life.

I know this from personal experience.

Starting out in my professional life, I thought I was doing everything the right way. A good job at a big Fortune 1000 company, with an impressive title and an office with a window. Check. I'm all set, and life couldn't be better, or so I thought.

And all of that's fine if that's what you really want, but if you've got the entrepreneurial bug in your DNA, you'll get antsy quick. (My guess is if you're reading this right now, then you know what I mean.)

To me, all the hype about the "grown-up life" was a lie. You do a good job, work longer and longer hours, sit in more and more meetings, and end up spending more than you make.

But hey, I got a plaque and certificate of appreciation!

I wanted more than a plaque, a warm place to sit for 8–9 hours a day, a 401k, and a cost-of-living raise every year. I consider myself fortunate to have found out early in my career that I wanted more and was willing to go get it.

Early Warning Signs

Ever since I was a kid, I've had the "be my own boss" itch. Remember the kid in your neighborhood carrying around a bucket wanting to wash your car, or going door-to-door offering to cut your grass for a few bucks over the summer and on weekends? . . . Yup, that was me.

And it didn't stop there. At 12 years old I had a crew of neighborhood kids going door-to-door selling our services. We were a growing enterprise. During the week, I hustled selling pixie sticks and bubble gum in the lunch room—a venture not looked upon too kindly by teachers.

There's a saying: The C and D students own businesses, and the A and B students end up working for them.

I'm living proof that there's validity to this statement. I'm not ashamed to say I barely made it out of high school and left university before they could kick me out. Meanwhile I was working, learning about business on my own, trying new things, taking risks, taking action, and getting results. Over the years I've had other ventures. You name it: selling advertising to local shops, web design services, multilevel marketing companies selling everything from gas rebates to groceries online. Some good, some bad, some profitable, some not, but . . .

All Learning Experiences

One of the keys to being an entrepreneur is to be willing to fall forward and do it fast. I'll admit my first major business attempt after leaving college was a major flop. And I'm thankful for it, because I discovered a lot about myself and the people around me—and that was positive.

I was in my early 20s and thought I was unstoppable. I knew it all, and I could do it all. I had a steady job working for a web development company that I had helped bring from the ground up, but I got bored and wanted more. (You'll see this is a pattern for entrepreneurs.)

So I quit—with nothing lined up. To add to the urgency, I had planned in two weeks to propose to my high school sweetheart and girlfriend of six years. (She said yes, by the way.)

The next year was filled with uncertainty and total confusion about what I should do next. I filled my days getting my hands on every course, book, CD, and seminar I could to learn how to make my business work.

I took on odd projects. We lived off the income of my new fiancée's first-year teacher salary and racked up thousands on the credit cards using advances to pay the rent. I even traded my services for gift certificates to a restaurant.

Yes, I worked for food, literally!

I often tell people that the worst thing that can happen if you go out on your own and it doesn't work is you have to get a job.

Well, that's what I did. And because I had spent a year developing skills, learning, and growing my ability to add value to the marketplace, I had made myself more valuable in the workforce. This landed me into a prime position using my new skillsets to open options that a college dropout like myself otherwise would not have had available.

But by now you know how I feel about working for someone else; as soon as I could, I ventured on my own again, and this time with . . .

Newfound Confidence and a Solid Game Plan

Through my experience, I created a game plan of exactly what I would want my business to look like and what it would take in time and resources.

My new goal was to create a business that supported my life, and not the other way around. I can fortunately say I've thrown out the conventions of traditional business and operate quietly under the radar while still being able to create a fantastic lifestyle for my family.

Here are a few key lessons I've discovered that have allowed me to fulfill my personal and business goals:

Attitude: There's a thin line between success and failure. Winners push despite past failure, they learn from every experience, and they use the past to fuel the fire to succeed.

Communication: Your ability to communicate and influence applies in every area of business—working with vendors, team members, and clients, and of course in making sales.

A strong network: Your network equals your net worth. It's often said that your income is a direct result of the five people you spend the most time with. I'm a natural introvert, but I've ignored my natural tendencies so that I could build a strong network of top-level players.

A support system: Stop listening to negative people in your life—they won't serve you or help you reach your goals. I've been blessed with a wonderful partner; my wife has been supportive every step of the way. In addition, the people I've attracted in my network all share similar goals, and that only serves to push us forward.

A mentor: I've been fortunate to have worked with many people I consider mentors. This is the ultimate shortcut to success, finding someone who has what you want, who has done what you're doing, and who has a proven path to reach your goals.

A business vehicle: What many don't realize is that there is so much opportunity just waiting for the armed and ready entrepreneur. You can take your own skills and fill a need, or plug into a ready-built system. If the system works, do it.

Risk: The willingness to take calculated risks is a requirement. Fear stops many people from achieving their goals, but the best way to overcome fear is to face it dead on.

Leverage: Here's the key to freeing yourself from work. Outsource: leverage time and other's resources. If you don't like doing a repetitive task, don't do it. If you can easily train someone else to take some work off your hands, do it. You'll have more time to work *on* your business.

Know Your Reason Why

Your reason why is the driver behind everything you do, especially if your goal is to create a lifestyle-driven business.

My reason why is to enjoy time with my family without having to worry about financial restraints. I've been fortunate to be a part of almost every second of my brand-new baby girl's life and watch her grow every day.

This is the lifestyle I've dreamed, by design. And now that you know it's possible, I hope you take time to figure out what matters most to you and live your dreams.

Biography
Francis Ablola

FRANCIS ABLOLA is a marketing strategist and award-winning business writer. His unique ability to effectively communicate with and influence wide audiences has generated millions in revenue and created tens of thousands of new opportunities for his clients. From Fortune 1000 to garage startups, he has been helping companies succeed using highly effective yet unusual advertising.

For effective marketing strategies that get results, visit www. AblolaDirect.com.

Contact Information

www.AblolaDirect.com

Chapter 27

Living in the Green
FROM THE LOVE BUSH LEAF
TO BUSH JUMBIES UNMASKED

by V. Celeste Fahie

"Living in the Green" in a book about the art and science of success? You're probably thinking this means I live a prosperous life, debt-free, and full of wealth. Hmmm. Well, actually, I live in the green. In the bush. But I hope after you read this, you will agree that a green life is a prosperous life.

I'm a native New Yorker born in Harlem to a Caribbean household. Ask me to describe myself in one word: Creative. My creativity has been my major source of success and the "one" thing I want to leave as a legacy to my family. If you asked the people who know me (and I know everyone) to describe me, here's what they'll say: artist, speaker, creative, storyteller, trainer, poet, educator, puppeteer, visual voice, talented, passionate, writer, headliner, knowledgeable, likes animals, nice smile—anyway, like I said, creative.

On September 16, 1995, Hurricane Marilyn hit St. Croix in the U.S. Virgin Islands, and my first house (built of wood) was destroyed. After the storm, when people would see me smiling, they would say, "You're smiling so you must have made out all right through the storm." When I would tell them my story, they would be shocked. My reply was always "You can rebuild but you can't rebirth." You see, two of my daughters (I have three) and my first grandchild lived together on this island, too, elsewhere. I was married at the time, and my husband and I weathered out the storm in what I thought was a relatively safe place until I witnessed firsthand the extent of the damage taking place on the outside. I prayed. I prayed hard, not for my house, but for my daughters and grandchild to get through their first hurricane safely. My prayers were answered.

Just days later I wrote a poem about "The Love Bush Leaf," a leaf of Caribbean folklore tied into magical growth, survival, and reproduction and used as a healing herb.

Years later, I realized this poem was about me. My survival, my ability and willingness to grow despite the many challenges I have encountered, and my insistence on trying to help others do the same. I believe that one person, alone, can make a difference or at least begin a parade.

I started this life in the advantage lane, an only child (so I thought) to middle-aged parents. My parents were entrepreneurs, talented and respected in the community where we lived. My father had my name tattooed on the wall of the building that housed his carpentry shop. My mother and I ran the family-owned candy store, right across the street from my elementary school, and I had my own key. My father played the piano and guitar and sang the Calypso songs he wrote. My mother was an active member of several movements for the civil rights of African American people. She attended her Caribbean, cultural, social, and political meetings often with me by her side. Lumber A. Grant described my mother in a letter entitled "Commemoration of a Community Brave Heroine and Unsung Patriot in Harlem": "Sister Fahie (Madam Fahie), as she was affectionately called by organizational colleagues, was a dedicated worker and charismatic speaker."

When I was a child, my mother told me stories about the Pied Piper and Humpty Dumpty, relaying messages to me: Don't be mislead, and choose wisely, because repair and recovery from the wrong choice is not always possible. She told me that I was as good as everyone else, but not better than anyone, that I was their equal. When these two busy parents couldn't make time for me, I had my aunt Daisy. She was a warm and welcoming homemaker, short in stature and big on morals. In my early years, my aunt, her son, my parents, and I all lived together for a while. So I was ready to lead the parade, with art, creativity, storytelling, speaking, a business mindset from my parents, and a warm, welcoming attitude from my aunt. I was set, right?

The headline that has gained the most global attention about me were written in a press release entitled "From Juvenile Delinquent to Successful Entrepreneur." Juvenile delinquent?! What happened? Long story short, my parents separated at a crucial time in my life, as I was entering my adolescence. My life was turned upside down. I went from honor roll student to runaway, suicidal, a resident in juvenile detention centers and public housing, teen parent, high school dropout, early bride, welfare recipient, divorced, and "surprise" sister to the now world-famous blind gym teacher Steven Sloan, who carried the torch for America in Italy for the 2006 Olympics.

"Girl, you just crazy." Maybe, but guess what? I never stopped creating. Even in the lowest times, perhaps especially at these times, that visual voice shone though my spoken word artistry, my free style of dancing, and my art.

Before my mid-twenties, I began the shift back to the positive, encouraged by my mother, who had returned to school after retiring, and her relationship and motivational attitude toward my brother (a new acquaintance to her also). I was determined to regain the spotlight. A parent of three beautiful girls, I was on my way back; with a high school equivalency diploma in hand, off to college I went.

BAM! My first husband died from sclerosis of the liver in his mid-twenties. It floored me. We were parents of my first child, married, and divorced. I had moved on, so why was I floored? I thought that I extremely disliked him, that I was over him, that the only love I had related to him was my daughter—I loved her not him. But I realized he was my story too.

He was smart, talented, handsome (to me), funny, had great handwriting (like our daughter). He was so much more and yet his life was full of pain. Had I caused any of this pain? Possibly some, but definitely not all.

My creativity increased. I wrote poems and letters (now lost), and I realized my path needed more adjustment. I thought, *I want to leave a positive legacy for my girls, and I never want to live this type of pain again.*

So I dedicated myself even more to college, a life that was great for me. My ability as an artist and as an art critic was recognized in my first semester. My creativity dominated throughout my college years: I worked on publications, internships, and apprenticeships that culminated in a double major degree, a bachelor in marketing and graphic arts. I moved on into the amazing world of corporate advertising, and I continued my education in the arts and business, finding a way to combine the two until eventually they were in sync. Then while working as a creative coordinator on a major account, I suffered an occupational injury, leaving me labeled as permanently partially disabled. Just around that time, I decided that I wanted to help produce better people rather than products.

?BAM! Another paradigm shift I became facilitator of the Network in the Schools program, working with students, parents, faculty, and the community. In using the powerful words to help others in this program, I affirmed my own future. I am… My dream is… I like myself because… My concerns are… My short range doable plan is. . . . A moment of silence for reflection, please. "I'm clear" became my primary daily phrase.

With my newfound clarity, I acted on another dream. I moved to paradise! I had been visiting the Virgin Islands since childhood, and I already lived the stateside Caribbean lifestyle. So my thought was, "Many people work all year long to save up enough money to spend two weeks vacationing in the Virgin Islands or on a Caribbean island—I'm going to live it." You know, the vacation lifestyle. "Girl, you just crazy!" Isn't this where I started? Sort of, but without the relationship history. Okay, I won't take you through the relationship stuff (stories!), but let's just say my relationships have lead to my jewels, my children, and that challenging experiences inspire great poetry, plenty of training material—on parenting, domestic violence, money matters, immigration issues, life skills, humane education, and for so many more—excellent topics for me to speak on.

But we all need new sources of inspiration, right? In my new paradise home, I reconnected with the stories I'd heard growing up about Jumbies.

Huh? What's a Jumbie?

Jumbies are spirits, but they are funny, or at least the stories about them are. Stories about these mischievous spirits are told in a West Indian dialect. Now I perform stories, write poetry, and lecture on the history around them, a history that is so diversified that it crosses into the cultures of Africa, Asia, Europe, the Caribbean, and America. *Bush Jumbies Unmasked,* the name of my art, spoken word, storytelling, and educational series, marks the ancestral conversations (often oral) of a history passed along from one generation to the next. Through this project, I have found out about grandparents I never met. My maternal grandmother was a storyteller, and my paternal grandfather may have been a Jumbie. "Girl, Stop it! you are crazy." Sigh. Anyway, living in the bush has provided me with the resources to use in making masks.

Success. I have created my success, happiness, and legacy through my vision. My life works—well! I am healthy, and my medicine cabinet is in my front yard, bearing names like noni, soursop (graviola), anamu, aloes, oranges, grapefruit, passion fruit, mangos, papaya, acerola cherries, and bush for morning tea. I make my living using my creativity as an artist, a professional speaker and trainer, and a life skills coach. I inspire others in multiple ways, working toward humane education in schools and in the community, holding workshops in prisons and empowerment workshops with women. My creativity also allows my entrepreneurship to flourish in business and in my leisure. I conduct historical tours, perform as a storyteller, recite poetry, and put on puppet shows. My newest creative project is U.S. and Virgin Islands prosperity roses.

In the past, *challenges* were my catalyst to create, but I had help: the creator, my spirituality, my family, the elders, mentors, historians, writers, poets, speakers, and authors on positive thinking. (The list is endless, but to name just a few: Aesop Fables, Og Mandino, Les Brown, Oprah, and Matt Morris.) Then my will, persistence, and determination to succeed became my *opportunities* to create. Now my desire to leave a worthy *legacy* for my descendants provides the love for me to create.

Am I successful? A moment of reflection, please. Yes! However, I am just getting started. I have a 95-year-old aunt, Ida Keeling, who is making history on the track as a sprinter to caught up to. So, I am successfully affirming my future and my creative legacy. I'm clear!

There they are. Pond lilies
bright & beautiful, refreshing to see
supported by what appears to be a leaf
as brilliant as the lilies themselves
all so refreshing that it makes
the pond now appear vibrant, alive;
No longer dark and murky
as the water that sits in a pond; still, quiet,
almost motionless, stagnant.
No Caribbean blue water here to gaze upon
No waves moving to and fro on banks of a shoreline
to listen to. Not here.
Only deep dark still pond water
Sometimes murky, always lifeless
Or so you thought
Until today when the Lilies arrived.

(© by V. Celeste Fahie, April 18, 2010)

Biography

V. Celeste Fahie

V. CELESTE FAHIE is a creative, colorful, passionate, energetic, down-to-earth, witty personality who uses her multiple talents to empower people and audiences into action. She moved from her native New York to paradise, the U.S. Virgin Islands, to live in the green and experience a lifestyle she had always imagined.

Ms. Fahie's will, persistence, and determination to succeed became her incentive to create. She has turned obstacles into opportunities: once labeled a juvenile delinquent, she is now respected as a successful entrepreneur with a national and international following. She says, "My success is my creativity, expressed through various art forms, inspired by my imagination and my experiences in life."

Visit www.vcelestefahie.com to learn more about her, her work, her e-book, and to download her poem on the love bush leaf.

Contact Information

www.vcelestefahie.com

livinginthegreen@vcelestefahie.com

Chapter 28

Infinite Possibilities through Sacred Partnership

by Bettie Spruill

*E*arly in life, I had an awareness that the way I thought life was, was not the same for everyone. In fact, there were many points of view, some of which I agreed with and others I did not. I considered many points of view wrong, and the ones that were right matched how I thought. The right points of views, the ones that matched mine, gave me great pleasure, and the ones that did not, based on my investment in the truth of them, left me, quite often, feeling anger and disappointment.

A large part of my journey in life was to find the "right" answers, especially for happiness and success. The more I searched for these answers, the more disappointed and frustrated I became. Having the "right" relationship didn't make me happy. Having the corner office, titles, and money didn't give me the feeling of success I longed for.

Even the experience of seeking a relationship with God and the Divine was disappointing. The sense that there was always something missing added to my overall experience of lack and insufficiency.

The older I became and the more I traveled, it appeared as though everyone was seeking happiness, success, and fulfillment through obtaining something: power, pleasure, self-improvement, spiritual attainment, or the simply the acquisition of more and better things. The overriding mantra was, *Someday when I have . . . , I will be successful and happy.* Countless leaders and teachers broadcast the news of acquisition for success and happiness.

That was my worldview of what was occurring until I had a larger understanding of worldviews, paradigms, contexts, and the power of interpretation and meaning.

Being born and raised in the United Stated shaped my worldview about success, love happiness, leadership, about all my interpretations of God, Self, the Universe—in essence, who I say I am, and how I shape my life. Until I understood certain aspects of the Western worldview, I could not understand myself in a way that gave me any freedom to shape or author a life of success and connection.

Mechanistic and Scientific Worldview

This is the perspective based on the understanding of the world by dominant figures in the West like Aristotle, Copernicus, Galileo, Descartes, Bacon, and Newton. In the sixteenth and seventeenth centuries, the medieval worldview based on Aristotelian philosophy and Christian theology changed radically. The notion of an organic, living, and spiritual universe was replaced by that of the world as a machine, and this world machine became the dominant metaphor of the modern era.

This view of the world added to the notion of separation and the experience of isolation and alienation that has come to represent the West. I am in here, and everything else is out there, leading to the subject/object duality and longing for connection in so many people. That which is real (exists) is determined by a set of laws that are fixed and immutable. These laws can be discovered, and when they have been discovered, we will understand once and for all how the universe works.

The mechanistic/scientific worldview tends to be exclusive and is great for making machines, but not necessarily good for an organic, living, spiritual universe. This worldview gave birth to the Industrial Revolution and has taken us into outer space and into the technological and information ages. Thinking directed in this way has no capacity to deal adequately with domains of interconnectedness, creativity, and God. Scientists have constructed reality according to form and dimensions and linear mathematical relationships. Leadership and success in this worldview is linear and based on control, order, and prediction. Not very much possibility.

The Emergence of the Quantum and Ecological Worldview

At the end of the nineteenth century, the Age of Reason was in its prime. The perception of the Universe as a machine was being debunked, and Newtonian physics was replaced by quantum physics and ecology. One by one, the rules of the scientific/mechanistic worldview lost their claim to certainty (truth) and were set aside to be used only selectively in special circumstances. The principles that form the new paradigm emerged.

Some of the old rules underwent transformation and became new principles. For example, the rule of separate time and space was transformed by Einstein's work into the principle of space-time, not separate but distinct. The concept of multiple worldviews in the quantum/

ecological paradigm contributed to my freedom and full self-expression. This principle allows for and embraces acceptance, diversity, and compassion. Embracing this principle challenges the entire notion of right and wrong. The emphasis is on the entire field of interconnectedness and relationship, making possible a new identity of ourselves as more than victims of the world. We become co-creators and leaders, and we have an understanding of ourselves as authors.

The emergent worldview of the twenty-first century places us in a unique sacred partnership, and our possibilities are constantly expanding. We discover in this worldview a new kind of respect for the power of what it means to be human. We partner with a power that is both sublime and forceful.

The subject/object duality of the mechanistic/scientific worldview places us in opposition to the world and its inhabitants. It even appears as if the world is coming at us, and therefore the world is already there, and we either love it or hate it. This perception sees others as being "over" and "there" and against us. The emerging worldview sees others as extensions of who we are, revealing to us ourselves.

With a principle of oneness, we finally awaken to the most profound and most meaningful awareness we can have for both success and leadership. We have an awareness that our deepest Self, our true Self, is whole, perfect, and complete. In our wholeness there is not an experience of lack, insufficiency, or scarcity. Our possibilities are as infinite as we are.

In the new paradigm, our commitment is to self-awareness and mastery, and we realize that awakening is both the journey and the prize. We are partners in the sacred, forever graced and embraced by it, intimately and eternally linked to all possibilities.

Self-mastery in this new worldview is a process that takes place in five stages:

1. We choose to be present.

2. By being present, we experience ourselves as the Source of our experience, and we communicate to connect and share.

3. Authentic responsibility shifts us away from any kind of blame or credit and into intentional creation.

4. Accepting and embracing ourselves and our results allow us to develop compassion for the human condition while maintaining true vision.

5. Living life by the principles of the sacred generates a field of trust and excellence and a partnership that is infinite.

Resting fully in the present is the source of happiness and success—and self-mastery. Once we open to our own wholeness, there is nothing to get; there is infinite space in which to express and create.

This thinking about worldview is not by itself revolutionary, and not even new. Many cultures have understood the illusory nature of worldviews. What is new is the pervasiveness of this thinking. The postmodern worldview is disclosing the "possibility of being" in radical and transformative ways.

Worldviews have been compared to the lens we wear with which we create our world. "We see the world the way we are, not the way it is." Shifting our worldview from that of machines to that of the sacred and quantum world that is constantly expanding is exciting and is inclusive of all life.

We construct new definitions of success and leadership based on partnership. Each period of history reveals more truth about us as sacred creators. Now is the time for sacred partnership.

Biography

Bettie Spruill

BETTIE SPRUILL, CMEC, is a sacredpreneur, a public speaker, an ontological coach, and a writer with over 30 years' experience in the field of transformation and wisdom teachings. She is a featured speaker in the film *The Answer.* Bettie's international coaching certification program has trained ontological coaches around the world. She holds a vision of leadership based on the principles of the sacred and commerce.

Contact Information

www.bettiejspruill.com

www.sayyess.com

Chapter 29

Commit to Success

by Esteban Srolis

Many people think about being successful. Do you believe that you are a successful human being? Are you committed to success? Have you defined success for yourself? Are you keeping your word to take action to be successful?

For me, success is just a combination of mentality and commitment. You choose moment to moment to create satisfaction and good fortune, to be complete in all areas of your life, and to act on your choices. Success is essentially a choice.

So if you decide to choose success, prove yourself. Be consistent no matter. See everything as an opportunity and always ask yourself, *What can I learn about this event, this conversation, this situation?* Keep each experience with you for the next step in your life.

Envision how success would look in your life. What steps can you take to make this vision come true? To consistently strive for it in your life or business?

1. Believe that you *are* a successful human being. If you believe it, you increase the possibility of it happening.

2. Define what success is for you. You must know exactly what you want if you're going to get it.

3. Create a vision consistent with your definition of success. Be clear about what are you creating and where are you going.

4. Be sure that your vision includes as many people as you can imagine. There is no way to create something alone. If you choose to have, you must choose to give. This is the universal law of abundance and prosperity, leading to a win-win game.

5. Make a list of what you choose to do and how you choose to be to create your vision. Successful people always have ways of being and acting that allow them to access success. You want to distinguish those ways of being and follow their example.

6. Take action. Follow through on your list of what you choose to do and how you choose to be. It's a simple equation: Thought + Action = Result. Be rigorous to coordinate your thoughts with your actions.

7. Ask for feedback on whether you are who you say you are. If you are, people will recognize it and see your success. If you aren't, you will need to shift based on this feedback to become the person you want to be.

8. Make sure every action you take is consistent with your vision and adjust if necessary. Remember that there is never just one way to do something. There are always many ways to get what you have chosen and want.

9. Ensure that you are satisfied in life, that you feel fortunate and complete. If you do, you are living your vision. You are successful.

All this sounds great, but we are all only human. It's easy to get stalled talking and thinking and planning. If we don't put our feet on the ground, even when the path to success isn't much fun, we can't realize success. Sometimes, we don't act because we don't think we have the money to pursue our path to success. But money won't come to you unless you do act. Realize that roadblocks like money are not real. They are just a mind conversations, and you have the power to shift these conversations by taking consistent action. Choose a conversation about success that confirms abundance is around the corner and act consistently with this new conversation. Shift the paradigm that says you have to *have* so that you can *be* and *do*. First choose to be, then take action doing what you choose, and *then* you will have what you want.

Another roadblock is time, thinking we don't have the time to pursue success. My first mentor, one of my best friends and my partner, once told me, "Time is just a concept. Time doesn't exist." After a long and serious investigation into what time is, I realized that all human beings on this planet have 24 hours each day, including the people who are successful. Time is just an excuse, an illusion in which we live; it is a mind conversation that we can choose to shift, so do it. Take action and create the life that you want.

Your life is full of challenges. That will not change, but successful people transform challenges into strengths that launch their actions directly toward their vision. This is possible by just asking the question I mentioned earlier: "What I can learn from this?" This powerful question gives to you the ability to create knowledge and your personal and exclusive know-how—that is priceless.

Much related with success is the big word leadership, but can you learn to lead, or are you, you born with it? It can be both or neither. I propose that you can choose it. Yes, it's your decision. It's your call.

From my experience, leadership is just a way of being that enrolls others in the vision you are committed to create.

When I write "enroll," I don't mean convince. I mean that others feel your vision as their own so they are committed to do whatever it takes to make that vision come true. They choose for your vision to be their goal or vision too; they are inspired, touched by the vision, and they develop a true and solid commitment to it.

If you choose to become a leader, you will need to access some important qualities. First, of course, you need the vision of what you want your life to be; then you have to commit to it in a way that's transparent, honest, communicative, and consequent with your vision. Decide and choose a win-win game for your life. See yourself as a success. This will bring you the great opportunity not just to create success, but to continue to live it. If you create a connection between your thoughts, your actions, and your language, you will have created the most solid and sustainable context for the success in your life. *Be* what you say you are, and this will let you shine as a complete human being because your mind, your heart, and your actions will completely align toward your vision, creating your successful life.

To keep you on the path to success, choose a mentor or many of them. They are like the radar for the airplane. They keep you on course, giving you constant and important information about the results of the actions you take. I have chosen many mentors. Your choice will depend on what you need to stay on track toward your vision.

When I chose my first mentor, I asked him to help me learn the skills that would support my vision of success. The information he gave me allowed me the opportunity to design the context of what I became; it helped me to answer a lot of my internal questions and create new powerful conversations that allow me see my paradigms as an opportunity to work on new ways to act in my life. Then I decided to have more mentors, each one of them giving me feedback about what I'm projecting in my life and whether that is consequent with the vision that I declared, whether I am who I say I am.

So if you want a successful life, be clear that your decision and your commitment alone will create it. You are no different from others. If you trust yourself as a successful person, your commitment and consistency will transform your life into one of extraordinary abundance and prosperity. 100% commitment = 100% results.

Biography

Esteban Srolis

ESTEBAN SROLIS's life was transformed 100% when he chose to commit to a vision that inspired him and called him to action in each moment. His vision has allowed him to work in different countries, meet extraordinary people, make new friends, have new and great life and business opportunities, and work as a transformational coach and trainer and finance adviser, two activities that give him the opportunity to help everyone transform a regular life into a success life.

Contact Information

www.estebansrolis.com

entransformacion.blogspot.com

committosuccess@estebansrolis.com

787-672-3099

Chapter 30

My Long Road to Glory

by Reverend Vincent Ezekiel Medina

I am a Mexican American man who comes from a family of 10 children. I grew up mostly in the Aliso Village Projects, just east of downtown Los Angeles. I lived the latter half of my life in East Los Angeles. Both areas are considered the ghetto. To survive in this environment, one must be tough and resilient. Our family survived by learning how to defend ourselves in the challenging environment of gangs, drugs, and crime.

Money was scarce and even nonexistent at times. Dad was a laborer and Momma was a stay-at-home mom. As children, we had limited ways of thinking since our parents had only a minimal education. Dad went to the sixth grade and Mom went to the eleventh. Survival was the first order of the day. Life was a day-to-day existence without any frills. We scarcely had enough food to eat or clothes to wear. Those were the things of importance.

As a child I never dreamed of being anything in life. I felt that poverty and desperation were all there was in life for poor people like us. I never dreamed of being a firefighter, teacher, policeman, or anything else. I became streetwise, letting no one take advantage of me, and finally graduated from high school. I was the first of 10 brothers and sisters to get a high school diploma.

In 1968 I entered the U.S. Marine Corps. Boot camp was a tough, grueling, and demanding experience for me, but I learned discipline and became a man really fast. I was sent for a tour in Vietnam from 1968 to 1969. In Nam I experienced the fear of death and the value of life. I learned then and there that life was a pearl of great price.

After returning from Vietnam, I went to work on a dock as a teamster loading and unloading forty-foot trailers. The job was physically demanding on every level. After 10 years of dock work, I became a truck driver. My route was smack dab in the center of downtown Los Angeles. The traffic was brutal, and the parking was worse. I had to make deliveries and pickups all over downtown, up and down hundreds of alleys and elevators delivering and picking up freight. The driving job proved to be hell on wheels, but somehow I stuck it out. I could swear that at times I felt like a paid slave, but being a Marine had made me steadfast and strong. Quitting was not in my constitution.

In 1972 I began listening to a program about successful thinking. When I heard Dr. William Hornaday and Dr. Frank Richelieu, both religious science ministers, teaching the science of mind, a seed was planted. I now knew that my life could be better. As I listened intently, I began to dream that I could be a success in life.

I enrolled in East Los Angeles College and graduated in 1977 with an associate of arts degree. All this time, however, I continued to listen to the science of mind teachings, and I had an intuitive feeling that one day I too would study this science.

After 17 years, my laborious job as a truck driver finally ended. The company closed its doors because of the economy. At that time I decided that I'd never work such a hard job ever again. I landed a job driving a city bus, which I liked. I was always clean and dressed sharply in a bus operator's uniform. My shoes were always shined to a high brilliance. No more hard labor for me. I had applied for other jobs at the same time that I applied for the bus operator position, and I was very surprised and happy when after a year, the Los Angeles Unified School District called me and asked me if I was still interested in working for them. I answered yes immediately. I sensed that I would love working for the school district.

My job in the district's maintenance department consisted of moving furniture, books, chairs, and so forth. Nothing too heavy like on the dock. We also did many small repairs at numerous school sites. With a great desire to advance, I took various classes to improve my skills. I took preparing for promotion and developing a professional image, supervision and management. I also studied and got my planning certificate. I could now plan jobs done by our department. My supervisor liked the way that I wrote, so he asked me if I'd like to work in the office planning jobs for a couple of weeks. I did such a good job in the office that I ended up working there for over a year. In that time I worked with supervisors, coordinators, teachers, and principals. I was a very good communicator.

It turned out that my hard knock experiences had been an asset. Everything that I had learned in my life began paying dividends. I eventually left the office and went back to work in the field with the maintenance department. It was not long before another job opened: senior tool keeper. My supervisor told me that our director had hinted that he wanted me to work in the tool room. Amazingly, I love working with tools, so I had studied about tools at the library years before, when I was between jobs. It was sort of uncanny the way that played out. I came out number one on the written test for senior tool keeper and aced my interview. I was interviewed by the area director and got hired on the spot.

In the interim I had been studying self-help books. The first great book that inspired my road to success was *Psycho-Cybernetics* by Maxwell Maltz. His book is literally a manual on how the human mind works. Dr. Maltz made it clear that our minds are goal-striving mechanisms like heat-sensing missiles. Once a missile of this type hones in on its target, it makes a direct hit. This was one of the greatest clues in knowing that I too could successfully reach my targeted goal.

I studied Dale Carnegie's *How to Win Friends and Influence People.* His book focused on strategies for communicating with people effectively, stating that we must take the other person's needs and wants into account when we deal with people. To be successful, we must be aware of this very important element. *The Power of Positive Thinking* explained how being positive has an almost magical magnetic effect of drawing success to ourselves. Norman Vincent Peale demonstrated that the majority of successful people are affirmative and positive by nature.

I read voraciously, at least a hundred different self-help books. It was my passion. It has been my road to success. I believe the easiest way to become upwardly mobile and successful is to read, read, and read. I eventually began to study the science of mind, as my intuition had implied that I would years before. The science of mind would be my destiny.

The science of mind teaches one *how* to think, not *what* to think. It has been said that at least 90% of the population thinks erroneously. They think in ways that limit their health, happiness, and success. Learning to think affirmatively and correctly has made my life a joyous unlimited experience.

I ultimately had a divine calling to study the ministry. My ministry class was held in Granada Hills, California. There were about seven students in the class, a few of them highly educated, with master's degrees. After a couple of years of study, we had a big test that is the crux of ministry. The test was all essay questions and was supposed to take about five hours. I passed the test in half the allotted time. My ministry teacher thought that I had failed because I had left the test room so early. She thought that the test had been too difficult for me and that I had given up. Her assumption proved wrong. I had completed and passed faster than any other student in class. Everyone in class was astonished. One student, who had been a rocket scientist on the Galileo project years back, told me that he was completely blown away by my accomplishment on the exam. It turned out that I got a pretty high score too.

Today I am a successful religious science minister, teacher, and profound public speaker. I preach gratitude, health, love, peace, and joy. I am very adept at teaching the principles of successful living. I've owned my home for 33 years. I am financially solvent and have aspirations for a mega church that will lift thousands of people to success by teaching the profound science of mind principles. My wife and I have four very intelligent, respectful, and productive children. My son is a successful real estate broker with a thriving business 25 employees strong.

I am still a zealous reader. Every chance I get I am reading. I've studied the lives of many great men like Abraham Lincoln and Theodore Roosevelt, who despite challenges and obstacles have made substantial contributions to humanity. The majority of successful men and women have been readers. Reading opens new vistas and visions for us.

Dare to struggle. Dare to Win.
—Unknown

To be winners, we must be grateful for every little thing in our lives. The universal laws of good are activated to a higher level when we are grateful. There is a divine connection in gratitude. We must also be bold and stalwart in our conviction to reach our goals. Life favors the bold. It favors the one who is strong enough to step out in faith with a can-do attitude. We must trust the process and principles of success to be fruitful in our quest. To be successful, we must be willing to work hard for as long as it takes to succeed.

The rule of thumb for success is never, never, never give up. A Chinese proverb says, get knocked down seven times, get up eight times. We are spiritual beings having a human experience. It is important that we go within and ask our source of inspiration for what we desire. Many of us just fail to ask for what we desire. If we do our part, success will follow just like night follows the day. There is a road map to success, and you can follow it. You just have to find it.

Biography

Reverend Vincent Ezekiel Medina

REVEREND VINCENT EZEKIEL MEDINA is currently teaching the science of mind as a staff minister at the Montebello Center for Spiritual Living. He is a public speaker in any venue, bilingual in English or Spanish, and does healing treatment work for any illness. Reverend Medina also officiates weddings, performs Quinceañeras, and does special yearly memorial services for loved ones who have made their transition.

Contact Information

vincent.medina@lausd.net

323-804-5966

Chapter 31

Journey to Success

by Crystal Wolfchild

$\mathcal{I}$ am a Dakota woman. I was born December 20, 1981, at home in Burbank California, surrounded by crystals, in the hue of a blue light. I emerged as Crystal Dawn Wolfchild. I was fortunate to grow up nurtured by loving parents who raised me in balance between the modern and traditional worlds. My connection to the Creator and Mother Earth grounded and supported me since the beginning. My first sweat lodge ceremony was at eight weeks, and sundance ceremonies blessed my summer months. At four years old I was given my spirit name, Morningstar Woman. The teachings of my ancestors, the Star Nation, guided my life. With my strong foundation, I knew that success was at hand. Little did I know that success had many different faces.

It wasn't until my father told me the stories of my people that the harsh realities set in. We were on a road trip one summer, passing through Mankato, Minnesota, where Dad told me of the 38

Mdewakanton Dakota Men who were executed in 1862. This was the largest mass execution in the history of the United States and nobody seemed to know it! The stockade was built specifically to drop all 38 men at the same time, and when it came time on December 21, the original hanging date, they didn't have enough rope to hang all of them at once, so Lincoln rescheduled for the day after Christmas. On that day, the townspeople came, families, women, and children, to witness the gruesome event. My whole world was struck; pain coursed through my body and hot tears flooded my soul. I was in disbelief. . . . How could this happen and why?!

If that wasn't bad enough, Lincoln ordered two more men kidnapped and hanged a year later, and one of the men was my grandfather Medicine Bottle. I didn't know what was more disturbing, that this travesty had taken place or that it was never talked about, taught in schools, or acknowledged. I was outraged. My mind racing, my body aching, millions of questions flooded my world. How can we praise Lincoln for freeing the slaves but fail to mention that he also ordered the hanging of 38 men the day after Christmas in 1862? This was but one of many historical events that aren't recognized . . . much less healed.

This knowledge was a huge part of my awakening. I realized the historical trauma, and a deep depression within the psyche of native people. I recognized the mental constructs and the depth of this wounded paradigm, from which my people were acting from, resulting in alcoholism, high rates of suicide, health problems, and so on. Though I was not a statistic, I was heartbroken. I was seeing what was happening to my people, heritage, culture, and traditions. We were getting lost in the story of what had happened. I saw the story as a lie, and that peace lay within each and every one of us—humankind. This was a powerful breakthrough for me.

My heart yearned for the truth, which brought me to the next leg of my journey—healing, forgiveness, and wholeness. The year 2004 marked the beginning of a memorial horse ride, honoring the 38+2 men who were hanged in Mankato. Jim Miller, a Dakota man, had a dream, some people would call it a fruition, calling, or vision. Around the same time, I heard my own calling. Our ancestors and the universe were speaking, lighting a path to freedom.

On the memorial of the hanging, Jim rode on horseback with many riders to Mankato. Four days they rode for reconciliation and forgiveness, to heal the past and honor the men and families whose lives were deeply affected. To heal those lives that are still affected today. The horse ride was a huge success. It brought the people together in a common goal. To be Dakota is to walk in peace with all living things. We were coming home to what is true.

My vision mirrored that of the horse ride and Jim's dream. My healing of personal hurts and trauma came through the sundance ceremony and transformational work. Everything was leading me back to spirit and my truth. What I learned through the transformational work was that to heal, I had to accept what is, harvest the lesson or gift that was birthed out of the event, and release and let go of the past—move forward like the buffalo. I could stand in the truth of what is now, the present, and what has always been. The beauty and power of what it is to be Dakota, to be alive, to be a human being in this magnificent world!

So-called history comprises events that happened in a time, in a place. I realized I was the creator of the meaning of that event and from which certain belief systems were born. The freedom came by knowing that the events happened, but that they did not define me, or take anything away from me as a native woman. I realized I had a choice! I could choose to be a victim and let something in my past take over my life and make me angry, sad, and depressed, or I could choose peace, and live my personal truth and divine right, to be joyful, free, and prosperous. I know who I am today, and I honor the past because I choose to see the beauty and gifts within. I get to be the change I want to see, to walk in peace with all living things, to stand in my principles of unconditional love, unity, peace, and joy!

Today as I write, I am much more than a Dakota woman . . . a spiritual being, an artist, a lover, a friend, a teacher, a student, and a powerful, courageous, passionate, loving woman. I choose in any moment who I am and what I want to create, through me, in me, as me. . . *being* whatever I declare. I choose a life of unlimited possibilities from which anything can be accomplished.

In my life I do many things, and although they are all significant, they do not define me. Or make me who I am. One of my passions is the art of makeup application. I remember as a child playing in my mom's makeup. I was the four-year-old Picasso! Brilliant, I tell you! Okay, maybe not brilliant in technique at age four, but that fire fueled my passion for working on the live canvas and brought me to a successful career as a makeup artist. My credits and acknowledgments could prove my "success," but no award nor credit proved my success to me. It was the embodiment of love, joy, and gratitude that showed me what success really is.

Success is doing what you love, what lives in your soul. It can be BIG or small—neither is more significant as long as you are living your personal truth. Never settle for mediocrity—if that is the way the cookie is crumbling, check within! You might be pretending not to know something and be doing what you think is the "right" thing. After all, there is no "wrong" or "right." Your results will speak for themselves. They say that if you want to know what your intention is, take a look at your results. If you don't like something, do something different! Whatever you do, do it 100%, whole heartedly. Do what inspires you, ignites your soul. Trust and listen to your body; it will never lie to you. Follow your bliss; your heart will lead you! Let your spirit be your guide, and all the abundance and prosperity will follow as a result of following your true nature.

Today I choose to be an artist, authentic and true to creating art on a live canvas. I work on people of every shape, color, and size, each uniquely beautiful and perfect. I found adventure in the entertainment world and began my makeup journey at age 19, fresh out of high school. In the past 10 years, I've been fortunate to have worked on TV and film such as *American Idol, Nip/Tuck, Heroes, America's Got Talent, So You Think You Can Dance, CNN's Larry King Live, Superhero Movie, School For Scoundrels,* and many more. I have been nominated for two Emmys for *So You Think You Can Dance* and received a First Americans in the Arts Award for Outstanding Achievement in Technical Arts for Makeup! I know that I have created these results for myself because I love what I do. I continue to listen to the song of my soul, and it leads me where I go next. That is where my current new business, OMGoddess Beauty, will teach woman all over the country and the world the art of self-expression through makeup. I live in gratitude for my abundantly ever-prosperous career and have many visions much bigger for the world.

I am forever grateful to keep expanding and expressing my life's dance . . . and to be a leader in the evolution of the planet through love. Through the history of my people, I realized that life wasn't perfect, that everyone has a story to tell, that everyone has hurts and sadness but also victories and triumphs of overcoming. That no matter the history or the story, human beings are resilient, creative, unique beings. Whatever happened in the past does not define or determine who we are, who we ever were. I stand in a space of who and what I choose to be in this moment. I am and have always been a success, because I have always had love in my heart.

Biography

Crystal Wolfchild

As a visionary innovative makeup artist and spiritual being, CRYSTAL WOLFCHILD stands for a world of infinite possibilities. A creative force in the makeup world, Crystal is the recipient of a First Americans in the Arts Award for Outstanding Achievement in Technical Arts for Makeup in 2008 and has been nominated twice for an Emmy award for her work on *So You Think You Can Dance*. Her unique style and exquisite talent has reached top shows such as *American Idol, Nip Tuck, Heroes*, and the *Superhero Movie*. She has worked with talent, such as Kelly Clarkson, David Cook, Cat Deeley, Julian McMahon, Chris Brown, Tiffani Thiessen, Hugh Laurie, and many more.

Besides living her true passion as an artist, she exemplifies leadership in her community by being in service through love, prayer and transformational work. One world, one heart, one love is her mission through her business OMGoddess Beauty, in which she teaches woman all over the country and the world the art of self-expression through makeup application . . . expressing within and throughout!

Contact Information

omgoddessbeauty.com

wolfchildcrystal@yahoo.com

Chapter 32

Working Consistently on the Right Path

by Edward Kinyanjui

*There are **no limitations** in what **you** can do **except**
the limitations of your own mind. . . .*

*The need not to look foolish is **one** of youth's many burdens; . . .*

*Develop your willpower so that **you** can **make** yourself do what **you**
should do, when you should do it, whether you feel like it or not.*

—Brian Tracy

I was born July 20, 1977, in the central part of Kenya, Kiambu district, the first-born son of two brothers. We were a middle-income family. My mother was a teacher and my father a construction supervisor. I attended a local primary and high schools, graduating with an above-average score, which qualified me to attend the prestigious Strathmore school of accountancy in Nairobi, Kenya.

One of the most defining moments in my life was my parents' role in my upbringing. They always impelled me to maintain my integrity regardless of the situation. One good example is after writing for my primary school exams, despite being the fourth in my class, I was admitted to a local day school that was one of my last-choice options; my dad insisted that since that was what I achieved, it would be where I went. Since that moment it was clear to me that despite any influence my parents had in our community, they would not allow any shortcuts or favors.

This is what prompted me to take the initiative to apply for admission to Strathmore long before I completed high school. To my surprise, I received an interview invitation just days after conclusion of my high school exams. This was the turning point in my life because immediately at the start of the following year, I was enrolled in the university while the majority of my schoolmates opted to wait for their results. At the young age of 21, I had completed my CPA qualification, and within two weeks of concluding my last exams in college, I had received a job offer with one of the most reputable organizations in Kenya. This was not due to luck, but a result of *planning ahead and taking action.*

Once employed I quickly rose through the ranks to a position of finance manager, and this was when I faced the greatest challenge. As I rose through and received recognition among peers and industry heads, I started to get other attractive job offers. The most difficult time to make rational decisions is when you are winning, and it is so easy to be complacent and ignore small details. I switched jobs, doubled my pay, and ventured into a completely different industry with a different work culture. After a period of 11 months, I was fired from my job, an eventuality that I never even dreamed of. It was the most devastating period in my life considering I had also just started to venture into real estate. I had just taken a bank loan to develop a property and had pegged the loan repayments from my salary. Having lived an almost automatic life, this at that time appeared to be the biggest challenge of my life.

During one of my low moments, I stumbled on the book *How to Sell Your Way Through Life*, by Napoleon Hill. This opened my eyes to the fact that adversities are a cycle in life and obstacles are the things you see when you move your eyes off the target. With this realization, I pursued my real estate development despite the limited funds and aggressively started to look for alternative jobs; surprisingly, there were a lot of job offers although not at the same level as the previous one I had held. So I took up day jobs and temporary consultancies.

Through this period I realized the power of self-education and motivation. I started reading books by Napoleon Hill, Anthony Robbins, Robert Kiyosaki, Spencer Johnson, Matt Morris, and so forth. Since that time, I have always had a book for reading at any time or an audio CD to listen to in the car.

The real estate development stalled just at the foundation stage, due to the limited availability of funds and the fact that I had ventured into a project just from my dreams with no proper due diligence. It took another seven years to have the real estate dream come true, and that was long after I attained a stable job. But I had learned a few lessons:

1. If you set yourself goals and take action, they will come true no matter how long it takes.

2. Adversities are just but wake-up calls to avoid complacency.

3. It is very important to plan and conduct proper due diligence before undertaking any project.

4. Self-education creates fortunes.

5. The power of positive thinking and self-motivation is invaluable.

6. Wishes without action are like dreams that end when you wake up.

This particular period in my life led me to the realization that my destiny is in my hands. You cannot rely just on a job and then hope and pray that all will be fine. In this age, you have to create wealth through diverse means; hence my venture into business and expansion of my real estate.

Business requires a totally different mindset and relies mainly on:

1. Creating a proper business plan.
2. Creating a good team.
3. Having good internal control systems.
4. Marketing and communication.
5. Operating within legal framework.
6. Providing overall leadership.

I have successfully started and run two small businesses and am currently venturing into big business by partnering with like-minded people of diverse knowledge. I am confident that this will soon be a business listing in the stock exchange.

> *Leaders aren't born. They are made. And they are made*
> *just like anything else, through hard work. And that's the price*
> *we'll have to pay to achieve that goal, or any goal.*
> —Vince Lombardi

Leadership starts with a vision of where you want to go and believing in it so much that you can influence others to follow and work toward that goal. A leader must possess, among other traits:

1. Integrity
2. Hard work ethic
3. The ability to motivate others
4. Vision filtration

My role models are leaders who are able to transform others by writing books and providing motivational talks and discussion forums. This extends the saying that if you find hungry people, teach them how to fish, and if you can teach multitudes you have changed generations!

Biography

Edward Kinyanjui

EDWARD KINYANJUI is a certified public accountant with over 10 years' work experience in diverse industries. He has worked in information technology, tourism and hospitality, and currently works in telecommunications. He runs a restaurant business and has interests in real estate. Edward lives in Nairobi, Kenya, with his beautiful wife and two kids, a son (three years) and a daughter (three months). They are the pillars to his life balance, and they give him more reason to work hard every day. Edward's dream is to be able to be there for them as a role model and cheerleader in good and bad times and to have time to spend with them throughout his life.

Contact Information

edwardkinyanjui.wordpress.com
kinyanjuiedward@gmail.com
+254-73-572-0704

Chapter 33

Reaching Success
with Excellence

by Ellen Reid

It seems like every day, I wake up and there's something new and different about the industry I work in. And I don't mean some little change; I'm talking about something earthshaking, life changing, revolutionary!

Okay, maybe it's not every day; however it started a few years ago, and the momentum is most definitely building. I work in the publishing industry, specifically the self-publishing end of it. I've been involved in this exciting field since 1998, and I have seen what feels like (and in times past probably would have been) a century's worth of changes take place in just over a decade. These include things like digital printing, print on demand, and, most recently, e-books and readers.

However, one thing I have observed to be constant is that those authors and books that have been successful—and in fact, people who are successful in any area of endeavor, whether in their business or in their personal lives—are those that demonstrate excellence. I have made excellence the cornerstone of my success.

"Excellence" has become my mantra, my branding, and, actually, my way of life. I'm not saying that excellence will guarantee success; however, I can't imagine real success without excellence being a part of it.

I wouldn't say excellence has always been a part of my life, but it is something that was tempered in the fires of my life's adventures. My father was of the narcissistic persuasion, so no matter what I accomplished, it somehow became about him. I soon learned that he demanded perfection, which, even to this day, I don't believe is possible. However, I was continually striving to do better and better. I may have missed perfection, but I guarantee you, I developed a real track record of excellence.

As I grew and matured, pursuing studies in personal growth, I came to learn how to transform my feelings of frustration with my father's unattainable demands into positive motivation to excel. Whether in my first career in sales and marketing, where I rose up the ranks to international buyer, frequently being sent to Asia to develop products, or in my current consulting/book shepherding career, in which I have been acknowledged as the Beverly Hills Premier Book Consultant, I have found myself compelled to both produce excellence and encourage others to it.

Excellence is something of an interesting concept. People know it when they see it, but they may not know *why* they recognize something as excellent. In my work, there are certain definite guidelines for what excellence is *not*. For example, typos in a book are a sure sign of less than excellent work—and they erode the value of the message. So, for me, one major element of excellence is attention to detail. That can be reflected by a well-proofread galley, which is pretty evident to everyone, but also in subtle things like the amount of space between lines on a page (called leading, which is a term taken from the days of hand setting type with individual letters cast from metal, like lead, and adding a line of lead in between the lines) or the amount of space between letters, called kerning. (I have no idea why they call it that.)

Another thing—one of those changes I was talking about—is that computers instill a false sense of ability. Anyone with a computer and Microsoft Word can create what may look like an actual book. But it's not, which you can tell when you compare a page done in Word with a page done by a professional with a page layout program. This leads me to another big tip: Know when you can handle something yourself, and know when it will serve you to bring in a professional.

When it comes to excellence, professionals are worth their weight in platinum. Some people are great at some aspects of their work, mediocre at other aspects, and downright poor at others. So one key I've found for myself and that I share with clients is to really evaluate what's necessary for any task and determine which you can legitimately do yourself and which you need help with. I counsel people to be ruthless with themselves and not be afraid to admit there are just some things they're not great at. While there may be some sort of subtle message in our culture that says we're supposed to be able to do everything ourselves, in my experience, it's the very rare person who can do it all with excellence.

One of the things writers need to look at is the quality of their book. Even the biggest names in the business, authors who have made millions and published lots of books, will tell you that one of their greatest assets and allies is their editor. While you may not be an author, you most likely do write letters for your business. Make sure they are well proofread, by someone other than you if possible. Catch all the typos and make sure it looks good on the page, neither too high or too low on your letterhead. Make sure your point is clearly stated and what you are asking the recipient to do is specific.

Okay, I know you may not send a lot of letters, but I'll bet you send several emails each day. While some of the ideas above may not apply, do proofread your emails for typos and grammar. And make sure what you're saying is clear.

Back to my writing clients. Not only do they need to start with making sure their manuscript is in excellent shape; they need to have a powerful cover. This means they need to get a book cover designer, not the daughter of a friend of theirs who did very well in her college design class. Book design is a specialized field, and not every good graphic designer knows the ins and outs of book cover design. Ditto interior design. You would be amazed at the difference in readability when a good interior book designer gets hold of a manuscript.

You can translate what I'm saying here to your own life and business. If you are putting something out that represents you or your business—and I mean anything, from a wedding invitation to a printed brochure—make sure it's done right, by a professional if necessary, if you want it to reflect excellence. And do your homework; if you're looking for a professional, don't just pick the first name that comes up when you Google "graphic designer." Part of excellence is following up with samples of work and references from others who have used the person's services.

Another area that comes up for my clients is promotional writing. On books, that's everything from the title and subtitle to the back cover and the short author's bio. What I often have to communicate to my clients is that just because they can write an excellent book does not mean they can write the text that is needed to sell their masterpiece. Again, it's a matter of finding a professional who can articulate what you're offering in a way that potential customers will recognize as having value to *them*. My experience is that many—maybe most—people are so close to their message, product, or service that they want to tell everyone about all of it. A good promotional copywriter will be able to advise on how much needs to be said to generate interest, and how much is so much information that people will lose interest.

Bottom line, what I preach and what I practice is that the right resource people—those who demonstrate excellence—will contribute to my excellence. And that contributes to my success.

Which brings me to the question of what is success. When I was younger I thought success was easy to measure. It had to do with how much money you made. Then, after I had made a fair amount of money, I discovered that I didn't feel particularly successful.

So I began exploring success from the inside out, which involved things like spirituality and personal growth. Those explorations revealed many avenues that I am still considering and dealing with. This is a lot like peeling away layers of an onion in that there's always another layer to work through. I expect these pursuits to be ongoing pretty much as long as I've got a body and am here on this earth.

In the end, it was probably this inner questing that brought my awareness to excellence. I find that to have genuine satisfaction in my life, I not only need to have balance, but I also need to make sure I feel fulfilled by what I am doing. I am driven to do excellent work and to have my work reflect the excellence of who I am—and, in a very real sense the excellence of who we all are. I find great satisfaction in encouraging my clients to be more of who they can be.

I can't tell you how great it feels to hear from thrilled clients when they receive their book from the printer and hold it in their hands for the first time. In virtually every case, they tell me that it's far beyond what they had ever envisioned. They feel great, and I feel good because I know they have achieved something they can be very proud of—because it reflects excellence.

Biography

Ellen Reid

ELLEN REID is a book shepherd extraordinaire. Since 1998 she has been assisting authors in exceeding their dreams for an outstanding book they can be proud of and that stands up to any competition. Acknowledged as Beverly Hills' Premier Book Consultant, Ellen has built her career on excellence. She is the author of the award-winning *Putting Your Best Book Forward: A Book Shepherd's Secrets for Creating Award-Winning Books that Sell.*

Contact Information

www.selfpubexpert.com
ellen@selfpubexpert.com

To receive over $2,000 in free bonus gifts
for purchasing this book, visit

www.SuccessYouPublishing.com/gifts

CPSIA information can be obtained at www.ICGtesting.com
Printed in the USA
LVOW05s0400010314

375593LV00026BA/1312/P